Better English

Literacy Skills

2nd Class
Activity Book

Maria Reilly

educate.ie

Introduction

Better English is a series of six books aimed at improving literacy in primary schools. Each book includes a 30-unit literacy programme based on a comprehensive grammar scheme, a range of exciting, thought-provoking and imaginative texts, a detailed and challenging language programme and a structured, weekly assessment of pupil progress.

Features include:

- Systematically developed literacy skills programme
- Extensive vocabulary to enhance and extend pupils' language
- Thematic-based programme to facilitate multi-grade work
- Grammar scheme developed from 1st class through to 6th class
- An extensive range of text and poetry providing challenging and enjoyable comprehension exercises
- Structured spelling scheme as part of the assessment programme
- Topics that provide for an integrated literacy focus across the curriculum
- Weekly assessments including grammar, proofing, dictation and spelling
- Week-by-week pupil profile as a guide for pupils, parents and teachers
- Online guidelines and materials for teachers

Better English 1st Class and *Better English 2nd Class* feature a three-page, 30-unit pattern of work as follows:

- Page 1 Comprehension: stories and poetry developing understanding and response to text
- Page 2 Language: exercises focused on language use and on writing skills
- Page 3 Grammar/Sounds: challenging exercises prompting accurate use of language
- Page 3 Spelling: weekly review and profile of spelling based on the spelling programme

Editor: Susan McKeever

Design and layout: Philip Ryan Graphic Design

Illustrations: Sue King, Andrew Geeson

Cover illustration: Sue King

© 2013 Educate.ie, Castleisland, County Kerry, Ireland

ISBN: 978-1-909376-07-6

Printed in Ireland by Walsh Colour Print, Castleisland, County Kerry. Freephone 1800 613 111.

The author and publisher would like to thank the following for permission to reproduce photographs: Wikimedia Commons, Lorraine Fabre.

The author and publisher would like to thank the following for permission to reproduce copyrighted material: "The Crocodile's Toothache" from *Where the Sidewalk Ends* by Shel Silverstein, © 2009 Evil Eye, LLC, by permission of David Grossman Literary Agency Ltd; "Today I Had a Rotten Day" from *Revenge of the Lunch Ladies* copyright © 2007 Kenn Nesbitt. All Rights Reserved. Meadowbrook Press. Reprinted by permission of the author. "Santa Got Stuck in the Chimney" copyright © 2006 Kenn Nesbitt. All Rights Reserved. Reprinted by permission of the author. "Halloween Is Nearly Here" copyright © 2010 Kenn Nesbitt. All Rights Reserved. Reprinted by permission of the author.

Contents

Mrs Duck Meets Mr Fox

Mr and Mrs Duck were afraid of Mr Fox. He was greedy. He loved to eat ducks. "Mrs Fox had three cubs yesterday," said Mr Duck one day. "Now Mr Fox will need a bigger dinner for his family." Mrs Duck began to shake. She was scared.

The next day Mrs Duck went for a swim. The pond was frozen. She walked across the pond to the long grass. Out jumped Mr Fox. "Good morning, Mrs Duck," said Mr Fox. "You are just what I need today." Poor Mrs Duck was really scared. Suddenly she thought of a plan. "Good morning, Mr Fox," she said. "I hear you have big family now. Mr Duck is much bigger than me. He eats so much that he is a big, fat, juicy duck. He is exactly the duck you need to feed your new family. He is asleep at the moment, so come with me."

Mr Fox grinned. "What a stupid duck," he said. He followed Mrs Duck.

Mrs Duck walked across the pond to where the ice was thin. Mr Fox was big. As soon as he walked on the ice it cracked and the ice broke. Down fell Mr Fox into the cold water. "Crack! Crack! Crack!" said Mrs Duck. "Now who is the stupid one?" she said, as she flew away.

A   Answer the questions by filling in the missing words.

     Mrs Duck   Mr Duck   Mr Fox   cracked   three   fell   frozen   ducks

1. Who was greedy? _____ was greedy.
2. How many cubs did Mr Fox have? He had _____ cubs.
3. What did Mr Fox like to eat? He liked to eat _____.
4. Who was big and juicy? _____ was big and juicy.
5. What happened to the pond? The pond was _____.
6. Who had a good plan? _____ had a good plan.
7. What happened to the ice? The ice _____.
8. What happened to Mr Fox? He _____ into the cold water.

B   True (✓) or False (✗)?

1.	Foxes like to eat ducks.	✓	4.	Mr Duck likes to eat foxes.		7.	There was ice on the pond.	
2.	Mrs Duck was scared.		5.	Mr Fox had three fox cubs.		8.	Mr Fox was happy on the ice.	
3.	Mr Fox was scared.		6.	Mrs Duck met Mr Fox.		9.	Mr Fox ate Mrs Duck.	

C   Imagine... Draw a picture of the three fox cubs.

A   Write each sentence correctly. Add the missing word.

1. Mrs Duck was of Mr Fox.   Mrs Duck was afraid of Mr Fox.
2. The duck does like the fox.
3. I usually go bed at nine o'clock.
4. At school the is in charge.
5. The was shining brightly today.
6. I had pasta and sauce dinner.

B   Write the words that match the clues.

horse   robin   dog   squirrel   cat
cow   hen   fox   goldfish   swan

1.	bushy tail	fox	6.	pet that barks	
2.	big white bird		7.	jumps fences	
3.	chases mice		8.	collects nuts	
4.	gives milk		9.	orange swimmer	
5.	red breast		10.	gives us eggs	

C   All about me! Underline one word only.

I like   chicken   fish   cheese   **best.**

I enjoy   painting   reading   playing   **most.**

I go to bed around   seven   eight   nine   **o'clock.**

I think school is   hard   enjoyable   exciting.

I like   television   playing   shopping   **best.**

Draw the time you go to bed at.

5

A Say the word. Write the sound.

glare	adventure	declare	care	bare	future
picture	stare	nature	capture	creature	mare

–are sound		–ure sound	
glare			

B Name and colour. Use the words from Activity A.

b a r e

_ _ _ _ _ _ _   _ _ _ _

_ _ _ _ _   _ _ _ _   _ _ _ _ _ _ _

C Listen and spell.

1.		6.	
2.		7.	
3.		8.	
4.		9.	
5.		10.	

Score

Sammy Squirrel

It is autumn. Sammy Squirrel is busy. Winter will be dark and cold so Sammy is going to hibernate (have a long sleep). Sammy must get ready for his long sleep. He needs a comfortable nest, and food for winter. Sammy works hard all day. First he finds a nice big tree. There is a hole in the tree – perfect to build a nest in!

Sammy gathers leaves and pulls them into the hole. He makes a lovely nest. Sammy then goes out to look for nuts. He finds hazelnuts and beech nuts. Then he finds his favourite nuts – acorns – under the big oak tree. He brings the nuts back in his paws. He puts them away carefully. This is his nut store. Now and again during the winter, he will wake up. It will be cold outside. Sammy will not go out. He will eat nuts from his nut store. Sammy is tired after working all day. It is now time to hibernate. He eats his supper – two acorns, one beech nut and one hazelnut. Then he curls up in his cosy nest. He wraps his bushy tail around him. Soon he is fast asleep. Sleep well, Sammy!

A Answer the questions by filling in the missing words.

leaves   beech nuts   autumn   a tree   hibernate   bushy   hazelnuts

1. What time of the year is it? It is _____.
2. Why is Sammy Squirrel busy? He is getting ready to _____.
3. Where will Sammy sleep? He will sleep in _____.
4. Name two kinds of nuts he will eat. (i) _____ (ii) _____
5. What kind of tail does Sammy have? He has a _____ tail.
6. What did Sammy use to make his nest? He used _____ to make his nest.

B True (✓) or False (✗)?

1.	Sammy is a rabbit.	✗	4.	Leaves are good for nests.		7.	Sammy does not eat hazelnuts.	
2.	Sammy will sleep in a tree.		5.	Sammy ate all the nuts.		8.	Sammy loves to eat acorns.	
3.	Squirrels have nut stores.		6.	Leaves fall in autumn.		9.	Squirrels have bushy tails.	

C Imagine... Draw pictures of these.

1. Sammy Squirrel	2. Sammy's nut store	3. Sammy's nest

A Write the sentences in the correct order. Draw a picture of one story.

They are red and yellow.

It is autumn.

The leaves are falling.

1. It is autumn.

2. _____

3. _____

The children like them.

They are on the tree.

Look at the chestnuts.

1. _____

2. _____

3. _____

B Write the correct word.

is   are   some   all

1. There __are__ four seasons.

2. It _____ autumn when the leaves fall.

3. In winter _____ animals hibernate.

4. In winter _____ animals need food.

5. Spring _____ the next season after winter.

6. In summer _____ children _____ on holidays.

7. Many children have _____ pets at home.

Here _____ some autumn leaves.

C What am I?

squirrel   frog   deer   hedgehog   fox   owl

1. I have four legs. I am prickly.   hedgehog

2. I collect nuts. I have a bushy tail.   _____

3. I hoot. I come out at night.   _____

4. I can jump. I croak. I like ponds.   _____

5. I eat ducks. I have a bushy tail.   _____

6. I am in the forest. I have antlers.   _____

What am I?

A Make real words.

−amp   −and   −oop   −ay   −ip   −ack   −all   −op   −at   −it

hip	h_____	h_____	h_____	h_____
c_____	c_____	c_____	c_____	c_____
tr_____	tr_____	tr_____	tr_____	tr_____
p_____	p_____	p_____	p_____	p_____

B Colour by sound.

sounds like **ah**	sounds like **eh**	sounds like **ih**	sounds like **oh**	sounds like **uh**

man tip cup met stop can drip club kept top hand hit gut test cop sand whip hut less flop pan rip burst bent rot cap fit pup step pop

C Listen and spell.

1.		6.	
2.		7.	
3.		8.	
4.		9.	
5.		10.	Score

9

The Crocodile's Toothache

The Crocodile went to the dentist
And sat down in the chair,
And the dentist said, "Now tell me, Sir,
Why does it hurt and where?"

And the Crocodile said, "I'll tell you the
    truth.
I have a terrible ache in my tooth."
And he opened his jaws so wide, so
    wide,
That the dentist, he climbed right inside.

And the dentist laughed, "Oh, isn't this
    fun?"
As he pulled the teeth out, one by one.
And the Crocodile cried, "You're hurting
    me so!
Please put down your pliers and let me
    go."

But the dentist just laughed with a Ho
    Ho Ho,
And he said, "I still have twelve to go –
Oops, that's the wrong one, I confess.
But what's one crocodile's tooth, more
    or less?"

Then suddenly the jaws went SNAP,
And the dentist was gone, right off the
    map.
And where he went one could only
    guess...
To North or South or East or West...
He left no forwarding address.
But what's one dentist more or less?

A Complete the sentences.

the wrong tooth   a big mistake   his mouth   a toothache   crocodile   the dentist

I. The crocodile had _a toothache_   .

2. He went to visit _____.

3. The dentist climbed into _____.

4. The dentist made _____.

5. He pulled out _____.

6. The _____ ate the dentist.

B What do you think?

I. Tick the boxes. Is the poem...
   (i) funny? Yes ☐ No ☐ (ii) scary? Yes ☐ No ☐ (iii) clever? Yes ☐ No ☐

2. Tick (✓) two words that describe the dentist.
   clever ☐   silly ☐   unlucky ☐   brave ☐   kind ☐   cruel ☐

3. Tick (✓) two words that describe the crocodile.
   greedy ☐   angry ☐   clever ☐   mean ☐   hungry ☐   cruel ☐

4. Write the line from the poem that you like most. _____

5. Write two words that tell how you feel about going to the dentist.
   (i) _____ (ii) _____

C Imagine... Draw a picture of a crocodile showing its teeth.

A Write sentences. Use the words.

1. dentist/teeth   The dentist brushed his teeth.
2. dentist/chair
3. crocodile/teeth
4. opened/suddenly
5. tooth/hurting
6. jaws/snap

B Tick (✓) the correct boxes.

1.	Crocodiles are...	small		scary	✓	sneaky		strong	✓
2.	Monkeys are...	scary		silent		smart		slow	
3.	Giraffes are...	gentle		scary		tall		furry	
4.	Dentists are...	scary		helpful		strong		clever	

C All about me!

My name is _____.

I am now _____ years old.

My favourite animal is the _____.

Sometimes I visit the _____. (dentist, doctor, zoo)

I eat lots of _____. (fruit, sweets, meat, vegetables)

Draw your favourite animal.

A Choose and write.

Example: small   fat: I have a **small**, **fat** pencil

tasty	large	crispy	green	sweet	blue
frisky	pretty	graceful	chewy	tiny	nasty

1. horse: There is a _____ , _____ horse in the field.
2. lunch: I had a _____ , _____ lunch yesterday.
3. friend: My friend is a _____ , _____ dancer.
4. house: I do not like that _____ , _____ house.
5. eyes: _____
6. cake: _____

B Write and colour.

a bubbly, hot bath   a pretty, sweet pig   a large, interesting book
a lovely, sunny day   a grumpy, old lady   a big, spotty frog

a grumpy, old lady

_____

_____

_____

_____

C Listen and spell.

1.		6.	
2.		7.	
3.		8.	
4.		9.	
5.		10.	

Score _____

12

The Lion and the Mouse

Once upon a time a big lion was sleeping. A tiny mouse climbed up on the lion's tail. He ran across his back. He slid down his leg. He was having fun. Suddenly the lion woke up. He grabbed the mouse in his paw. "Please let me go," said the mouse. "If you let me go I will help you some day." The lion laughed. "You are so small! How could you ever help me?"

The lion laughed so much he had to hold his tummy. The mouse jumped out of his paw and ran far, far away. Hunters had left a trap to catch the lion. It was a big net made of ropes. The next day when the lion was out looking for food, he fell into the trap. He roared and cried but he could not get out.

The mouse heard the lion's roar and came to help him. The mouse began to nibble the rope. He nibbled and nibbled until the rope broke. The lion was then able to get out of the trap. He was free again.

The lion turned to the mouse and said, "Dear little mouse, I am sorry I laughed at you. You saved my life. You are a good friend. Thank you very much."

A Complete the sentences.

nibbled   climbed   trap   tail   lion   rope   mouse   paw

1. The mouse ____climbed____ up on the lion's _____.
2. The lion grabbed the _____ in his _____.
3. The _____ fell into the _____.
4. The mouse _____ the _____.

B True (✓) or False (✗)?

About the mouse...		About the lion...	
The mouse climbed up on the lion.	✓	The lion laughed at the mouse.	
The mouse was very cross.		The lion was very kind.	
The mouse was in the lion's mouth.		The lion fell into the trap.	
The mouse ran away from the lion.		The lion laughed when he was in the trap.	
The mouse was kind and helpful.		The lion said "Thank you" to the mouse.	

C Imagine... Read the poem and draw a picture.

A Lion Stole My Pencil

A lion stole my pencil, he held it in his teeth.
A lion with a pencil, too much, beyond belief!
He wrote a little note, then shook his golden mane.
He only wrote one word, that one word just read "pain"!
In his paw there was a thorn, stuck, despite his might.
He needed me to take it out, and that's why he did write.
At first I didn't want to, it seemed a dangerous chore.
But the lion then convinced me, when he began to roar!

13

Unit 4 - Language

A   Write each sentence correctly. Add the missing word.

1. The lion stole pencil.   _The lion stole the pencil._
2. It a sunny day yesterday.
3. I had chicken my dinner.
4. I would an ice-cream, please.
5. An apple has pips in the.
6. did you put my lunchbox?

B   Who lives in each home?

stable   house   field   kennel   burrow
water   cage   den   hole   nest

1.	a bird	nest	6.	a lion in a zoo	
2.	a fish		7.	a sheep	
3.	a dog		8.	a rabbit	
4.	a mouse		9.	a fox	
5.	a horse		10.	a person	

C   All about me! Underline one word only.

Today I had   soup   salad   milk   for lunch.

It was   wet   sunny   cold   coming to school.

I got up around   seven   eight   nine   o'clock.

I am wearing   boots   trousers   socks.

I would love a pet   pig   elephant   lion.

Draw your school clothes.

A Say the word. Write the sound.

rain   stile   mile   crocodile   chain   while

pile   brain   plain   tile   stain   pain

–ain sound		–ile sound	
brain			

B Name and colour. Use the words from Activity A.

t i l e

_ _ _ _

_ _ _ _

_ _ _ _

_ _ _ _

_ _ _ _

C Listen and spell.

1.		6.	
2.		7.	
3.		8.	
4.		9.	
5.		10.	

Score

The Clever Tortoise

An elephant and a hippopotamus lived in the jungle. They were good friends. A tortoise lived in the jungle too. He wanted to be friends with them. "You cannot be friends with us. You are too small," said the elephant. "You are too weak," said the hippopotamus. The two friends jumped into the water, splashed about and had fun.

"I am stronger than the two of you," said the tortoise. "Here is a rope. I will go in the water. You will not be able to pull me out." The elephant was angry. "Of course I can pull you out," he said. The tortoise swam into the water with the rope in his mouth. He swam to the bottom and tied the rope to a very big rock. The elephant pulled and pulled. He pulled again and the rope broke. Then the tortoise put the rope back in his mouth and swam to the top of the water.

"It is my turn now," said the hippopotamus. "Here is a new rope. You stay on the river bank. I will go into the water and pull you down." When the hippopotamus was under the water the tortoise tied the rope around a big tree. The hippopotamus pulled and pulled until the rope broke. He came up with the broken rope in his mouth.

"Now," said the tortoise. You see how strong I am. Would you like me to be your friend? "Yes," said the elephant. "We are safer to have you as a friend than as an enemy."

A Answer the questions.

1. Who was the elephant's friend? _____
2. Where did the tortoise tie the rope in the water? _____
3. What did the tortoise tie to the tree? _____
4. Which animal was the most clever? _____
5. Which animal got angry? _____
6. Which animal do you like the best? _____

B True (✓) or False (✗)?

The hippopotamus...		The elephant...		The tortoise...	
was at the seaside		was very small		wanted to have friends	
did not like the water		liked the hippopotamus		was very clever	
was friends with the elephant		played in the water		was very strong	
had no friends		was very clever		tricked the elephant	
was very strong		was bigger than the tortoise		did not like the water	

C Imagine... Draw pictures of these.

1. the elephant   2. the hippopotamus   3. the tortoise

A   Write the sentences in the correct order. Draw a picture of one story.

This is its home.

It has a hard shell.

The tortoise moves very slowly.

1. The tortoise moves very slowly.

2. _____

3. _____

Then we had ice-cream.

We saw the lion.

We went to the zoo.

1. _____

2. _____

3. _____

B   Write the correct word.

will   were   was   where

1. We __were__ at the zoo yesterday.

2. It _____ a lovely sunny day.

3. We went to _____ the lion lives.

4. He _____ asleep.

5. _____ do the tortoises live?

6. I _____ find them the next time.

7. We _____ tired at the end.

C   What am I?

donkey   mouse   goat   lion   tortoise   giraffe

1. I have a shell. I am slow.   _____tortoise_____

2. I am a fierce cat. I am a king.   _____

3. I am small. I have a long tail.   _____

4. I like carrots. I live on a farm.   _____

5. I have a long neck. I am tall.   _____

6. I live on a farm. You can drink my milk.   _____

What am I?

_____

Unit 5 - Sounds

A Make real words.

–ast   –ing   –all   –et   –an   –oat   –ade   –ay   –are   –ot

f_ast_	f_____	f_____	f_____	f_____
c_____	c_____	c_____	c_____	c_____
w_____	w_____	w_____	w_____	w_____
p_____	p_____	p_____	p_____	p_____

B Colour by sound.

| sounds like **air** | sounds like **ing** | sounds like **ape** | sounds like **ice** | sounds like **ace** |

air / grape pace slice sing chair / ape

lace rice wing pair cape place

ice / fling stair shape grace mice / king

fair drape race price thing hair

tape / face nice ring air shape / ace

C Listen and spell.

1.		6.	
2.		7.	
3.		8.	
4.		9.	
5.		10.	Score

Halloween Is Nearly Here

Halloween is nearly here.
I've got my costume planned.
It's sure to be the most horrific
outfit in the land.

If you should see me coming
you may scream and hide your head.
My get-up will, I guarantee,
fill every heart with dread.

And yet, I won't be dressing as
you might expect me to.
I will not be a vampire
or ghost that hollers "boo!".

I won't look like a werewolf
or a goblin or a ghoul,
or even like a slimy blob
of deadly, dripping drool.

I will not be a zombie
or some other horrid creature.
No, this year I'll be much, much worse...
I'm dressing as a teacher.

A Complete the sentences.

teacher   nightmares   Halloween   boo   vampire

1. It is almost Halloween   .

2. The poet will not be dressed as a   .

3. He will be dressed as a   .

4. The poet's costume might cause   .

5. The ghost hollers   .

B What do you think?

1. Tick (✓) the boxes. Is the poem…
(i) funny? Yes ☐ No ☐ (ii) scary? Yes ☐ No ☐ (iii) clever? Yes ☐ No ☐

2. Tick (✓) two words to describe Halloween.
scary ☐   exciting ☐   fun ☐   boring ☐   dark ☐   silly ☐

3. Tick (✓) two words the poet might use to describe the teacher.
tall ☐   grumpy ☐   clever ☐   kind ☐   funny ☐   scary ☐

4. Write the line that you like most.

5. Would you like to meet a real ghost ? Yes ☐   No ☐

C Imagine… Draw what you will look like on Halloween.

A Write sentences. Use the words.

1. costume/Halloween   I have a funny costume for Halloween.
2. scary/costume   _____
3. scream/ghost   _____
4. Halloween/vampire   _____
5. mask/teacher   _____
6. horrible/nightmare   _____

B Tick (✓) the correct boxes.

1.	Ghosts are...	fun		boring		real		white	✓
2.	Nightmares are...	scary		lovely		boring		fun	
3.	Halloween is...	dark		fun		scary		boring	
4.	At Halloween you see...	lions		pumpkins		sweets		worms	

C All about my teacher!

My teacher's name is _____ .

My teacher has _____ eyes.

Sometimes my teacher wears _____ shoes.

My teacher likes _____ .

My teacher does not like _____ .

Draw your teacher.

A Choose and write.

Example: intellegent, old   We have an **intellegent**, **old** dog.

awful   excellent   incredible   intelligent   kind   old
delicious   interesting   angry   amazing   furry   outrageous

1. magician: She was an _____, _____ magician.
2. animal: It was an _____, _____ animal.
3. told: My friend told an _____, _____ story.
4. me: I am a _____, _____ person.
5. book: _____
6. cake: _____

B Write and colour.

an angry, ugly insect   an unhappy, angry baby   an intelligent, ugly monkey
an exciting, old car   an awkward, old chair   an amazing, old book

an amazing, old book	_____	_____
_____	_____	_____

C Listen and spell.

1.		6.	
2.		7.	
3.		8.	
4.		9.	
5.		10.	

Score

Hiawatha

Long ago there lived an American-Indian boy called Hiawatha. His mother died when he was a tiny baby so he lived with his grandmother. He lived in a wigwam (a type of tent) in a forest beside a great lake. There were wild animals in the forest but Hiawatha was not worried. He was safe and warm in the wigwam.

At night his granny sang American-Indian songs for Hiawatha. When the moon shone brightly in the sky, his granny told Hiawatha American-Indian stories about the moon. When they looked up and saw the stars his granny told him American-Indian stories about the stars. Hiawatha loved the songs and the stories. He loved his granny too. He was a very happy little boy.

Hiawatha spent so much time in the forest and by the lake that all the birds and animals knew and loved him. As he grew older, he gave them all names. They loved to see him coming. The birds showed him how they built their nests. The beaver showed him how he built a dam across the river. The squirrels told him where they had their store of nuts hidden. The deer showed Hiawatha how fast he could run. Even the shy little rabbit was not afraid of Hiawatha. Hiawatha was loved by everybody.

A   **Answer the questions by filling in the missing words.**

boy   died   wigwam   baby   beaver   songs   squirrel   deer   stories   rabbit

1. Who was Hiawatha? He was an American-Indian _____.

2. Why did he live with his Granny?
   His mother _____ when he was a _____.

3. In what kind of house did he live? He lived in a _____.

4. What did Hiawatha like to hear? He liked to hear _____ and _____.

5. Name three animals that lived near Hiawatha.
   (i) _____   (ii) _____   (iii) _____

6. Which animal was shy? The _____ was shy.

B   **True (✓) or False (✗)?**

Hiawatha...		The animals...		Granny...	
lived with his granny		lived in the wigwam		looked after Hiawatha	
was an American-Indian boy		loved Hiawatha		looked after the animals	
lived near the seaside		sang songs at night		had nice stories	
had no friends		lived in the forest		had a nice wigwam	

C   **Imagine... Draw pictures of these.**

     1. the wigwam   2. Hiawatha's granny   3. the shy rabbit

A   Write each sentence correctly. Add the missing word.

1. Hiawatha loved grandmother.   Hiawatha loved his grandmother.
2. The little was very happy.
3. Why did take my lunch?
4. Please talking now.
5. I have a birthday for you.
6. this the pencil you lost?

B   Write the words that match the clues.

brother   grandmother   mother   dog   cat
lion   hen   duck   cow   sheep

1.	puppy	dog	6.	lioness	
2.	kitten		7.	calf	
3.	chicken		8.	sister	
4.	duckling		9.	father	
5.	lamb		10.	grandfather	

C   All about grannies! Underline one word only.

Grannies are cheerful old helpful.

They often have sweets glasses kittens.

They never shout dance cry.

They are sometimes tired grumpy sleepy.

They like children chips cheese.

Draw a nice granny.

A Say the word. Write the sound.

cape	stale	tape	female	shape	whale
sale	gape	male	scrape	gale	escape

–ale sound		–ape sound	
whale			

B Name and colour. Use the words from Activity A.

c a p e

_ _ _ _

_ _ _ _

_ _ _ _

_ _ _ _

C Listen and spell.

1.		6.	
2.		7.	
3.		8.	
4.		9.	
5.		10.	

Score

Fairy cake bake

Fairy cakes are tasty little buns to eat. It is fun to make them. It is also fun to pick the colours and shapes for icing the tops of the buns. Here is a simple recipe. Just remember these good-cook rules:

1. Ovens can be very hot. Be careful.
2. Do not cook without permission.
3. Make sure there is an adult nearby.
4. Do not forget any of the main ingredients.
5. Clean up – do not leave the kitchen in a mess!

Ingredients	Instructions
125 g soft butter 125 g caster sugar 125 g self-raising flour, sifted 2 eggs, beaten 2 tablespoons of milk **For extra special taste add...** **a little vanilla or thin grating** **from an orange**	1. Preheat the oven to 190 °C 2. Mix the butter and sugar. 3. Mix in the beaten eggs. 4. Mix in the sifted flour. 5. Mix in the milk. 6. Divide into about 16 bun cases. 7. Bake for about 12 minutes. 8. Take out carefully and allow to cool.

A Answer the questions.

1. Do you ever cook at home? Yes ☐ No ☐ What do you cook? _____

2. Name two ingredients you need for fairy cakes.

   (i) _____ (ii) _____

3. Write two important rules about baking.

   Rule 1: _____ Rule 2: _____

4. What two icing colours do you like on buns? (i) _____ (ii) _____

5. What special treat do you like:

   (i) for your lunch? _____ (ii) for a party? _____

B Quick Pick

True (✓) or False (✗)?		Making fairy cakes you need...		About myself...	
Fairy cakes are small buns.		125 g of butter		I like fairy cakes.	
Fairy cakes can have nice icing on top.		125 g of jam		I like chocolate buns.	
Cats and dogs eat fairy cakes.		to heat the oven first		I cook at home.	
You have to bake fairy cakes in the oven.		to eat all the cakes yourself		I buy buns in the shop.	

C Imagine... Draw pictures of these. 1. a fairy cake 2. a big birthday cake

25

Unit 8 - Language

A Write the sentences in the correct order. Draw a picture of one story.

I put icing on them.

I made buns.

Then I put them in a box.

1. I made buns.

2. _____

3. _____

Yesterday she made biscuits.

I ate two biscuits.

Granny is a good cook.

1. _____

2. _____

3. _____

B Write the correct word.

has   have   was   were

1. I __have__ a lovely Granny.

2. She _____ in our house.

3. We _____ all hungry.

4. We wanted to _____ buns.

5. "If you _____ eggs I will bake," said Granny.

6. I _____ really happy.

7. Granny _____ gone home but we still _____ some buns.

C What am I?

milk   crisps   bun   sweets   carrot   banana

1. I have pink icing. I am small. ___bun___

2. I am in a bag. I am crunchy. _____

3. I am in a packet. I am sweet. _____

4. I am a vegetable. I am orange. _____

5. I am a fruit. I am yellow. _____

6. I am a drink. I am white. _____

What am I?

26

A Make real words.

–ip   –ap   –at   –ay   –op   –ack   –eam   –ange   –and   –art

strip	str	str	str	str
ch	ch	ch	ch	ch
r	r	r	r	r
p	p	p	p	p

B Colour by sound.

cl sound	**ch** sound	**cr** sound	**ing** sound	**amp** sound

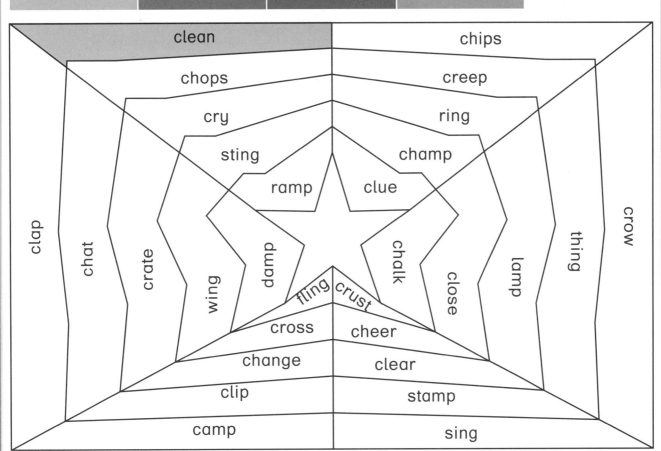

C Listen and spell.

1.		6.	
2.		7.	
3.		8.	
4.		9.	
5.		10.	Score

Santa Got Stuck in the Chimney

Poor Santa got stuck in our
   chimney.
I know it sounds weird, but it's
   true.
His feet made it down, but his
   belly
was one size too large for the
   flue.

His reindeer are up on our
   rooftop.
His sleigh is still loaded
   with toys.
And Santa, that kindly old
   fellow,
is making a whole lot of noise.

If you don't have presents this
   morning,
we're sorry you're having to
   wait.
But Santa's still stuck in our
   chimney.
   He may be a day or two late.

   Until then, please hide all
   your cookies.
Though Santa may find this
severe,
   at least then he'll fit down
   the chimney
   when he comes on
   Christmas next year.

A Complete the sentences.

children   stuck   reindeer   their   Santa   belly   chimney   rooftop

1. _____ got _____ in the chimney.

2. His _____ was too big to go down the _____.

3. Rudolph and the _____ were on the _____.

4. The _____ could not get _____ presents.

B What do you think?

1. Tick (✔) the boxes. Is the poem…
   (i) true? Yes ☐ No ☐ (ii) silly? Yes ☐ No ☐ (iii) funny? Yes ☐ No ☐

2. Tick (✔) two words that describe Santa.
   kind ☐   mean ☐   overweight ☐   hard-working ☐   foolish ☐   lovely ☐

3. Tick (✔) two words that tell how you feel about Christmas.
   excited ☐   greedy ☐   happy ☐   nervous ☐   bored ☐   delighted ☐

4. Write the line that you like most. _____

5. Write three things you would like from Santa.

   (i) _____   (ii) _____   (iii) _____

C Imagine…

   Draw a picture of a present
   you would like for Christmas.

A Write sentences. Use the words.

1. stuck/chimney   Santa got stuck in the chimney.
2. belly/Santa
3. rooftop/snow
4. reindeer/nose
5. toys/Christmas
6. noise/rooftop

B Tick (✓) the correct boxes.

1.	Christmas is...	boring		lovely	✓	exciting	✓	horrible	
2.	Santa has a...	red beard		sack		blue hat		happy face	
3.	Rudolph has a...	red foot		big ear		red nose		beard	
4.	I would like a...	surprise		bicycle		jigsaw		book	

C All about me!

I _____ Christmas. (love, enjoy, hate)

I hope I get _____ from Santa.

I _____ write a letter to Santa. (did, did not)

We will give Santa _____ and _____. (milk, cake, biscuits, tea)

We will give Rudolph _____ and _____. (water, carrots, sugar)

Draw a snack for Santa.

The yellow pencil is long.

The red pencil is even longer.

A Choose and write.

small   fast   hard   high   warm   nice
smaller   faster   harder   higher   warmer   nicer

1. The boy was _____ at running. His brother was even _____.
2. Mary got a _____ present. Anne got an even _____ present.
3. It was a very _____ day today. It was even _____ yesterday.
4. The homework was _____. Sums are _____ than reading.
5. Dad ate a _____ piece of cake. I ate an even _____ piece.
6. The horse jumped over a _____ fence. The next fence was even _____.

B Draw and colour.

cold, little boy and colder, little girl	small, brown dog and smaller, black cat	big, red apple and bigger, green apple
nice, yellow bun and nicer, pink bun	long, blue pencil and longer, red pencil	pretty, brown hat and prettier, green hat

C Listen and spell.

1.		6.	
2.		7.	
3.		8.	
4.		9.	
5.		10.	

Score

Asal has a baby

Shay and Maria are twins. They live on a farm near the beach. Grandad Leo is very kind and nice. He bought them two donkeys. Shay called his donkey Clip Clop. Maria called her donkey Asal. They played with the donkeys. Sometimes the donkeys raced each other. Asal was good at running and won most of the races. Clip Clop was gentle. He loved children. In

summer Dad and Shay went to the beach every day. Clip Clop gave donkey rides to children on the beach. Asal sometimes went to the beach with Maria. Asal would run on the beach. Asal was getting better and better at running.

Sometimes Shay and Maria gave treats to the donkeys. Clip Clop loved apples and Asal loved carrots. One day Mum and Dad told the children some very good news – Asal was going to have a baby! Shay and Maria were excited. They rushed to the shed. Maria got the sweeping brush. She swept the shed. Shay got fresh hay and put it on the ground for Asal. Then they got some apples and carrots. They also got sugar lumps as a special treat for Asal. One day Dad came to the school and brought the children home early. Mum was in the shed. She had a camera. "Look, look," said Shay. "Asal got her new baby." "It is a girl donkey," said Mum. "Wonderful," said Maria. "We will call her Asalín."

A Answer the questions by filling in the missing words.

kind   a farm   the beach   nice   the shed   Asal

1. Where do the twins live? They live on _____.

2. Where did Clip Clop work? He worked on _____.

3. Where was Asalín born? She was born in _____.

4. Which donkey was better at running? _____ was better at running.

5. What kind of person is Grandad Leo? He is _____ and _____.

B True (✓) or False (✗)?

1.	Clip Clop was a kind donkey.		4.	Shay was older than Maria.		7.	Clip Clop had a new baby.	
2.	Asal was quick at running.		5.	Clip Clop worked on the beach.		8.	The new baby was Asalín.	
3.	Grandad Leo owned Asal.		6.	Carrots were Asal's treat.		9.	Dad took photos of the baby.	

C Imagine... You have a camera. Show the photos you have of:

1. baby Asalín's bed   2. donkey treats   3. Grandad Leo

A   Write each sentence correctly. Add the missing word.

1. The children had donkey.   _____
2. You should always be to animals. _____
3. My lives in a kennel.   _____
4. I can my cat purring.   _____
5. We no homework today.   _____
6. I put on my bread.   _____

B   Write the words that match the clues.

scrambled   sandwich   bunch   crust   segment
mash   bag   leaves   finger   cake

1.	bread	sandwich	6.	icing	
2.	lettuce		7.	tea	
3.	grapes		8.	orange	
4.	ham		9.	potato	
5.	fish		10.	egg	

C   All about me! Underline one word only.

I prefer roast mashed chipped potatoes.

I enjoy rain wind ice most.

My friend has green blue brown eyes.

I am really good at sums reading writing.

My schoolbooks are heavy interesting lost.

Draw your friend.

A Say the word. Write the sound.

song	bang	sang	wrong	hang	long
rang	among	along	gang	belong	fang

–ang sound		–ong sound	

B Name and colour. Use the words from Activity A.

C Listen and spell.

1.		6.	
2.		7.	
3.		8.	
4.		9.	
5.		10.	

Score

33

All about libraries

Libraries are great places. Lots of schools have them and there are libraries in most towns also. It is nice to go to a library to look for a book. Some books are story books; others have poems and songs. Some books give information – about how things work, people long ago, about the weather and about plants and animals.

A librarian works in the library. A librarian keeps the books in the right place and helps to find the book you want.

There are rules in all libraries. These are some of them:

1. Libraries are quiet places for reading. Do not make noise.
2. You can borrow books for about three weeks. Bring them back in time.
3. People who keep books too long will have to pay a fine for each late week.
4. Take care of all books. Do not write on them or tear them.

In 2012 a library in Navan, County Meath had a late book returned to it. The book came back 80 years late! That is about 4,160 weeks later than the correct time. When the librarian came in on Monday morning somebody had left the book in the letterbox. Nobody wanted to pay the fine. The book was so late that the person owed a fine of €4,160. The person must have been really old if they came back after 80 years.

A Answer the questions.

1. What do you borrow in a library? _____
2. Name two types of books you can get. (i) _____ (ii) _____
3. What do you pay if you bring a book back late? _____
4. Write two important library rules.
   Rule 1: _____
   Rule 2: _____
5. How many years late was the book that came back in 2012? _____
6. What was the fine? €_____ Did anyone pay the fine? Yes ☐ No ☐

B True (✓) or False (✗)?

The lost book...		Some books...		Librarians...	
came back to Navan library		give lots of information		are helpful people	
was lost for only one year		have nice poems and stories		sell books to people	
was eaten by a dog		get lost or torn		help people pick books	
was missing for 80 years		do not like to be in libraries		keep books in the right place	
was left in the letterbox		are too hard to read		charge fines for late books	

C Imagine... Draw pictures of the covers of these books.

1. a book for babies   2. a book about a dragon   3. a book about animals

A Write the sentences in the correct order. Draw a picture of one story.

I was there yesterday.

I get them in the library.

I like books.

1. _____

2. _____

3. _____

Now I know a lot about them.

I read a book yesterday.

It was about cows.

1. _____

2. _____

3. _____

B Write the correct word.

did   done   was   were

1. I _____ all my homework last night.

2. I had _____ good homework all week.

3. The teacher _____ very pleased.

4. The teacher said we _____ all doing great work.

5. She told my mum that I _____ good.

6. Mum said she was proud of the work that I had _____.

7. We _____ all happy in the classroom.

C What am I?

football   whistle   balloon   goalie   footballer   grass

1. I am on a string. I can burst. _____

2. I am a player. I do not play in goals. _____

3. I am small. I can make a loud noise. _____

4. I am a player. I play in goals. _____

5. I am round and hard. I bounce. _____

6. I am green. Footballers play on me. _____

What am I?

_____

Unit 11 - Sounds

A Make real words.

–amp   –awl   –eep   –ay   –ip   –ack   –all   –op   –isp   –it   –ent

l_____	l_____	l_____	l_____	l_____
w_____	w_____	w_____	w_____	w_____
cr_____	cr_____	cr_____	cr_____	cr_____
sh_____	sh_____	sh_____	sh_____	sh_____

B Colour by sound.

ble sound	**eat** sound	**eep** sound	**ast** sound	**ar** sound

seat	star	eat	tar	cheat	bar
able	fast	fable	mast	gable	last
peep	creep	beep	weep	keep	sweep
cast	table	blast	cable	past	sable
car	meat	far	heat	scar	neat

C Listen and spell.

1.		6.	
2.		7.	
3.		8.	
4.		9.	
5.		10.	

Score [ ]

36

Sammy Snake's Grandpa

Sammy gives an admiring stare
At his old grandpa resting there.
For he is proud, for goodness sake,
To have him as his Grandpa Snake.

His stories make the young snakes
    smile.
So he keeps it up for quite a while.
Then they say, "It would be nice
If you could give us some advice."

Old Grandpa takes his glasses off,
He hums a hiss and gives a cough,
And says, "Young snakes, I'll tell to you
Some simple things I've found are true.

As Grandpa talks there are snake sighs,
Nodding heads and bright snake eyes.
For young snakes know that he is real
And seek the knowledge he'll reveal.

The secret of life is very clear.
Just care for others while you're here.
I know that I would crawl a mile
Just to make a sad snake smile."

Each night as Grandpa crawls in bed
Our little Sammy bows his head.
"Please give this gift: when I awake,
Another day with Grandpa Snake."

A Answer the questions by filling in the missing words.

> Grandpa Snake   a snake   nice grandfather
>   Young snakes   Sammy Snake   be kind

1. Who was Sammy? He was _____.

2. Why was he a lucky Snake? He had a _____.

3. Who wore glasses? _____ wore glasses.

4. Who was Grandpa's grandson? _____ was his grandson.

5. Who listened to Grandpa's tales? _____ listened to him.

6. What did Grandpa say? He said to _____ to others.

B What do you think?

1. Tick (✓) the boxes. Is the poem…
   (i) clever? Yes ☐ No ☐   (ii) scary? Yes ☐ No ☐   (iii) sad? Yes ☐ No ☐

2. Tick (✓) three words that describe Grandpa Snake.
   young ☐ wise ☐ selfish ☐ clever ☐ kind ☐ old ☐

3. Tick (✓) three words that describe Sammy Snake.
   proud ☐ angry ☐ worried ☐ mean ☐ happy ☐ young ☐

4. Write the line that you like most. _____

5. Write two words that tell what you think about snakes.
   I think snakes are _____ and _____.

C Imagine… Draw a picture of Sammy Snake and two of his friends.

A Write sentences. Use the words.

1. snake/hissed _____
2. snake/legs _____
3. Grandpa/glasses _____
4. sad/kind _____
5. old/bed _____
6. crawl/awake _____

B Tick (✓) the correct boxes.

1.	It is good to be...	kind		angry		helpful		cruel	
2.	Snakes...	crawl		hiss		walk		read	
3.	Dogs...	hiss		bark		jump		sleep	
4.	Cats can...	climb		fly		write		jump	

C All about me!

I would like a _____, _____ dog.

My dog would be _____ and _____.

I would give it _____ and _____ to eat.

I would give my dog the name _____.

I would teach my dog to _____.

Draw the dog you would like.

The brown crayon is dark.

The black crayon is darker.

A Choose and write.

smart   great   cold   bold   tough   bright
smarter   greater   colder   bolder   tougher   brighter

1. She was a _____ player. Her sister was even _____ .

2. It was a _____ snowy day today. It was even _____ yesterday.

3. The monkey in the zoo was _____ . He can sometimes be _____ .

4. My torch was very _____ . I think you can get a _____ one.

5. It was a _____ party. I will have an even _____ party.

6. It was _____ walking up the hill. Running up would be _____ .

B Write and colour. Pick two words to describe each picture.

sweet   old   helpful   gentle   little   yummy
kind   sticky   itchy   fat   tall   grumpy

tall , helpful	,	,
boy	cat	donkey
,	,	,
baby	bun	girl

C Listen and spell.

1.		6.	
2.		7.	
3.		8.	
4.		9.	
5.		10.	

Score

39

Tom and the Leprechaun

Tom really really wanted to find a leprechaun. His grandad told him if he found a leprechaun he would be rich. Grandad said the leprechaun was at the end of the rainbow. He said the leprechaun had a pot of gold. Grandad also said the leprechaun was very clever. One day Tom saw a rainbow. He followed the rainbow all the way to the end. He came to a wood full of trees. Tom heard a small tapping noise. "Tic-tac-tic-tac-toe!" He saw a leprechaun mending shoes. He lifted the little man up in his hand. "Good morning, leprechaun," said Tom. "I have found you. I want to be rich. Please give me your pot of gold."

The leprechaun walked with Tom to a tree in the middle of the wood. "The gold is under this tree," he said. "You have to dig it up and it will be yours." Tom knew he had to go home to get a spade. He had a yellow ribbon in his pocket. He tied the ribbon around the tree.

Tom knew the leprechaun was clever. "There are many trees here," said Tom. "Promise me you will not take my ribbon off the tree," said Tom. "I promise I will not touch your ribbon," said the leprechaun. Tom went home. When he came back with his spade each tree in the wood had a yellow ribbon round it just like his one. Poor Tom!

A Answer the questions.

 1. Who told Tom about the leprechaun? _____
 2. What was the leprechaun doing? _____
 3. Where was the gold? _____
 4. What did Tom put on the tree? _____
 5. What did the leprechaun do? _____

B True (✓) or False (✗)?

Leprechauns...		Tom...		The story...	
are at the end of the rainbow		was the name of the grandad		is about leprechauns	
are big and clever		had a ribbon in his pocket		is about Tom's granny	
have gold in their pockets		wanted to find the gold		is true	

C Imagine... Colour the leprechaun and draw the other pictures.

	Tom	the rainbow

A Write each sentence correctly. Add the missing word.

1. I have a tissue in pocket. _____
2. The leprechaun has a pot of. _____
3. are small people. _____
4. We were happy we the game. _____
5. Please do not that sweet. _____
6. I will my lunch with you. _____

B Match. Write the words that match the clues.

lunchbox   brush   playground   chair   copybook
bell   pencil   book   schoolbag   teacher

1.	you read it		6.	you put books it	
2.	you use it to write		7.	you listen to him/her	
3.	you write on it		8.	you hear it ringing	
4.	you use it to paint		9.	you sit on it	
5.	you put your lunch in it		10.	you go there for break	

C All about me! Underline one word only.

I like school football swimming **best**.

My teacher is kind helpful funny.

I find sums spelling writing **hard**.

After school I play sleep read.

I eat dinner at about four five six **o'clock**.

Draw yourself eating dinner.

A Say the word. Write the sound.

short	ship	champ	chain	shell	chest
change	share	shoe	chop	shining	cheer

ch– sound		sh– sound	

B Name and colour. Use the words from Activity A.

_ _ _ _ _ _   _ _ _ _ _ _   _ _ _ _ _ _

_ _ _ _ _ _   _ _ _ _ _ _   _ _ _ _ _ _

C Listen and spell.

1.		6.	
2.		7.	
3.		8.	
4.		9.	
5.		10.	

Score

Saint Brigid and the Fox

Saint Brigid lived in Ireland a long time ago. At that time there were kings in Ireland. The king of Ireland had a pet fox. It was a good fox. It was gentle like a kitten. It could do lots of tricks. One day the fox escaped and ran into the woods. A hunter killed the fox. The king was angry. The king told the hunter he would kill him. The man's friends went to visit Saint Brigid. They asked her to help. Saint Brigid went to visit the king. On the way she saw a fox in the woods. "Come with me, little fox," she said. All the animals loved Saint Brigid because she was so kind. The fox jumped into her arms. Suddenly he was kind and gentle like the king's old fox. When Saint Brigid arrived the king was still angry. "The hunter will be killed," he said. Saint Brigid smiled. "I have the best fox," she said. "He can do more tricks than the fox you lost." The king saw the fox doing his tricks. He was pleased. He took the fox and let the hunter go.

SAINT BRIGID	
☆ Saint Brigid lived in Kildare. People loved her because she was always so good and kind.	
☆ Saint Brigid's Day is on 1 February. This is also the first day of spring.	
☆ Many places in Ireland are named after Saint Brigid.	
☆ There are many schools in Ireland called Saint Brigid's school.	

A Answer the questions by filling in the missing words.

killed   Irish saint   fox   escaped   hunter

1. Who was Saint Brigid? She was an _____ .
2. What pet did the king of Ireland have long ago? He had a _____ .
3. What did the fox do one day? One day the fox _____ .
4. What did the hunter do? The hunter _____ the fox.
5. Who was the king angry with? He was angry with the _____ .
6. What did Saint Brigid bring to the king? She brought him a _____ .

B True (✓) or False (✗)?

The king...		Saint Brigid...		The fox...	
got a new fox from Saint Brigid		was afraid of animals		is a wild animal	
was angry with the hunter		was a very kind person		is a clever animal	
wanted to kill the hunter		visited the queen		can read and write	
had a pet tiger		lived in Kildare		lived with the king	
killed the hunter		has her feast day in March		was killed by the king	

C Imagine... Draw pictures of these. 1. the king   2. the fox

A Write the sentences in the correct order. Draw a picture of one story.

One day a hunter killed it.

The king was angry.

The king had a fox.

1. _____

2. _____

3. _____

Kildare is near Dublin.

She lived in Kildare.

Saint Brigid was a good person.

1. _____

2. _____

3. _____

B Write the correct word.

when   why   what   who

1. I saw you _____ I was shopping.

2. I know _____ you got in the shop.

3. _____ did the other person buy?

4. _____ did you not wait for me?

5. Tell me _____ you are going again.

6. I want to go with you _____ you go there.

7. _____ will you buy the next time?

C What am I?

tap   sponge   toothbrush   towel   shampoo   toothpaste

1. You squeeze me. You also taste me. _____

2. I help to get you dry. _____

3. You put me on your hair. I smell nice. _____

4. You turn me on. There are two of me. _____

5. You squeeze me. You use me in the bath. _____

6. I am important. I clean your teeth. _____

What am I?

A Make real words.

–amp   –and   –ap   –ay   –ip   –y   –ispy   –op   –aw   –ib

cr_____	cr_____	cr_____	cr_____	cr_____
cl_____	cl_____	cl_____	cl_____	cl_____
str_____	str_____	str_____	str_____	str_____
tr_____	tr_____	tr_____	tr_____	tr_____

B Colour by sound.

th sound	sh sound	ch sound	st sound	nt sound

bath	beach	bush	tooth	sent	cast
gush	mast	reach	hush	moth	teach
each	rent	frost	tent	went	crush
fast	cloth	flush	arch	past	strength
bent	path	mush	peach	last	meant

C Listen and spell.

1.		6.	
2.		7.	
3.		8.	
4.		9.	
5.		10.	Score

The Apple

1. I drew a little apple
but it looked so like a
    head
that I put a body on it
and it was a man instead.
I gave him arms and legs
    and hair
and eyes and mouth and
    nose
and I gave each arm five
    fingers
and I gave each leg five
    toes.

2. I put a row of buttons
down the middle of his
    coat
and just there right beside
    him
I drew a little boat.
The little boat was sailing
    fast,
the waves were big and
    blue
the seagulls flew around it
– as seagulls often do.

3. I looked at it, I liked it,
    and to myself I said
I think I'll draw an apple
now that isn't like a head!
So I drew a little apple
but it looked just like the
    sun
I put some sun beams
    around it...
I counted twenty-one.

4. The sun must shine on
    something
so I drew a little shed
and I gave the shed a
    chimney,
so it was house instead.

5. I drew a door and
    windows,
and a handle on the door,
I don't think I've ever
    drawn
as nice a house before!
And then just right beside
    it
I drew a little chair
And a table and a pussy
    cat
for people living there.

6. I looked at it, I liked it,
and then I said "For fun,
I think I'll draw an apple
now that isn't like the
    sun!"
So I drew another apple,
but it's near the end of
    day,
I'm tired of drawing
    apples,
so I'll put my pen away.

A What do you think?

1. Tick (✓) the boxes. Is the poem…
    (i) clever? Yes ☐ No ☐ (ii) enjoyable? Yes ☐ No ☐
2. What went down the middle of the coat? _____.
3. What went around the sun? _____.
4. Name three things that the house had.
    (i) _____ (ii) _____ (iii) _____
5. What two things could you draw that look like an apple?
    (i) _____ (ii) _____

B Read the poem again. Draw these verses.

1.	3.	5.

A Write sentences. Use the words.

1. coat/buttons _____
2. apple/seeds _____
3. boat/sailing _____
4. shed/door _____
5. sun/sunbeams _____
6. tired/now _____

B Tick (✓) the correct boxes.

1.	A house has…	windows		doors		kitchen		seaside	
2.	A boat sails…	in water		at sea		on land		in a lake	
3.	An apple has…	skin		bones		seeds		taste	
4.	I have…	2 eyes		1 tail		4 legs		1 nose	

C All about me!

I live in a _____ , _____ house.

There are _____ windows in the house.

The colour in my bedroom is _____.

The room I like best is the _____.

There are _____ people living in the house.

Draw your bedroom.

| **angry** | **angrily** | The lion was angry.
The boy angrily left the room. |

A Choose and write.

gentle   happy   peaceful   speedy   careful   greedy
gently   happily   peacefully   speedily   carefully   greedily

1. It was a _____ car. It _____ left the garage.
2. The clown was _____. He _____ laughed and laughed.
3. The baby slept _____. The house was _____.
4. The boy played _____ with the kitten. The kitten was _____.
5. The dog ate everything _____. It was a _____ dog.
6. Dad lifted the baby _____. You have to be _____ with babies.

B Write and colour. Pick two words to describe each picture.

crying   eating   sleeping   playing   running   walking
quickly   unsteadily   loudly   quietly   happily   greedily

playing   happily   _____ _____   _____ _____

_____ _____   _____ _____   _____ _____

C Listen and spell.

1.		6.	
2.		7.	
3.		8.	
4.		9.	
5.		10.	Score

Buses

Long ago only rich people had cars. People walked or used a bicycle to go places. Donkeys and horses brought people to special events. Buses were only seen in cities or big towns. Buses came to Ireland in 1927. They were single-deck buses – there was no upstairs part. Almost 80 years ago, the double-deck buses (also called "double-deckers") came to Dublin. These buses were exciting because people could go upstairs and look out the windows. The old buses were noisy. There was no door – just an opening in the back. If the bus had left the bus stop people would run after it and try to jump on. There were no seat belts. The bell was old. It needed a big bang to get it to work. The stairs were at the back of the bus. It was scary coming down the stairs. You had to hold on tight because if there was a big bump on the road you could fall down the stairs or even out the back!

THE BUS CONDUCTOR

On buses long ago, the drivers did not collect the fares. Instead, every bus had a bus conductor to do this work. The conductor had a bag for money and a special ticket machine strapped over his shoulder. Conductors walked up and down the bus calling "Fares please," collecting the money and printing tickets from the machine.

A Answer the questions.

1. How did people travel before cars and buses? _____
2. What was special about double-deck buses? _____
3. What was not in old buses? _____
4. Who collected the bus fares long ago? _____
5. What did the bus conductor have? _____
6. Did you ever go on a bus? Yes ☐ No ☐ Where did you go? _____

B Quick Pick

True (✓) or False (✗)?		Find the word...		Spelling scramble...	
Buses are only for rich people.		has two wheels		sub	_ _ _
Old buses had no doors.		you ring this		tkicte	_ _ _ _ _ _ _ _ et
Conductors collected the fares.		catch the bus here		refa	_ _ _ _
Conductors drove the buses.		collects fares		vrdier	_ _ _ _ _ _ er

C Imagine... Draw a bus stop. Put people standing at the bus stop.

A   Write each sentence correctly. Add the missing word.

1. The drives the bus. _____

2. You must a seat belt. _____

3. The school has four wheels. _____

4. The bus stops the school. _____

5. Be crossing the road. _____

6. You have to for the bus. _____

B   Write the words that match the clues.

driver   pilot   teacher   jockey   sailor
footballer   nurse   swimmer   farmer   mechanic

1.	hospital		6.	plane	
2.	pool		7.	horse	
3.	bus		8.	garage	
4.	school		9.	field	
5.	tractor		10.	boat	

C   All about me! Underline one word only.

I go to school by   walking   bicycle   bus   car.

I go to school with   Mum   Dad   a friend   a helper.

I like to travel in a   bus   boat   plane.

Once I went on holiday on a   bus   boat   plane.

I would love to fly in a   rocket   helicopter   hot-air balloon.

Draw yourself in a hot-air balloon.

A   Say the word. Write the sound.

stamp	spaghetti	sty	spy	stage	spot
space	stoop	spoon	stall	spring	stairs

st– sound		sp– sound	

B   Name and colour. Use the words from Activity A.

C   Listen and spell.

1.		6.	
2.		7.	
3.		8.	
4.		9.	
5.		10.	

Score

51

Friends Stick Together

Jeff and Tom were friends. They lived in the mountains, and loved going for walks in the forest nearby. Sometimes they would bring a picnic. There was only one thing they did not like about the forest – bears! "If any bear comes out of the trees I will stay with you and help you," said Tom. "I will help you too. After all, we are friends, and friends stick together," said Jeff.

One day Tom and Jeff were deep in the forest. They were having a picnic. Suddenly they heard a very large growl. They turned around and saw a great big bear. Up they jumped and started to run. Tom tripped and hurt his foot. Jeff did not stop. "Wait! Please help me," said Tom. But Jeff was afraid and kept running. He climbed a tree and was safe. He looked back and saw Tom.

Tom was on lying on the ground. Tom was afraid but it was too late. He pretended he was dead. The bear came over to Tom. He put his nose down and smelled him. He sniffed and sniffed. He thought Tom was dead so he went away. He turned back to the picnic table and ate the picnic. He went away happy. Jeff came down the tree and came over to Tom. "What did the bear say when he put his mouth near your ear?" said Jeff. Tom answered, "The bear told me to be very careful who I pick as friends. He said friends stick together, and not to bother with people who run away from you when you need them most."

A Answer the questions.

1. Who were friends? _____
2. Where did they live? _____
3. What did they hear? _____
4. Who went up the tree? _____
5. Was Jeff a good friend? _____
6. Name your two good friends. (i) _____ (ii) _____

B Quick Pick

True (✓) or False (✗)?		Find the word...		Spelling scramble...	
Jeff and Tom were friends.		big hills		pjudem	_____ed
Tom climbed a tree.		lots of trees		utnrde	_____ed
Tom pretended to growl.		growling animal		mcledbi	_____ed
The bear ate the picnic.		a meal outside		paphy	_____y

C Write three words that describe bears.

1. _____ 2. _____ 3. _____

A Write the sentences in the correct order. Draw a picture of one story.

Then you can go back home.

It is nice to have a friend.

You can play together.

1. _____

2. _____

3. _____

Then I go to bed.

Sometimes I watch cartoons.

I like watching television.

1. _____

2. _____

3. _____

B Write the correct word.

yesterday   now   tomorrow

1. I bought a book _____.

2. I will not be finished until _____.

3. I am reading it _____.

4. I saw another book in the shop _____.

5. I do not have the money to buy it _____.

6. Dad gave me money _____.

7. Maybe he will give me more _____.

C What am I?

cave   mountain   forest   field   stone   apple tree

1. I am quite dark. I have lots of trees. _____

2. I have roots and branches. I have fruit. _____

3. I am dark and cold. I am made of rock. _____

4. I am large and sloped. You can climb me. _____

5. I am small and hard. You can lift me. _____

6. I have grass. I usually have a gate. _____

What am I?

A Make real words.

-ate   -een   -oot   -ave   -ill   -ark   -ale   -op   -at   -in

b	b	b	b	b
s	s	s	s	s
h	h	h	h	h
sh	sh	sh	sh	sh

B Colour by sound.

cr sound	**tr** sound	**cl** sound	**bl** sound	**pl** sound

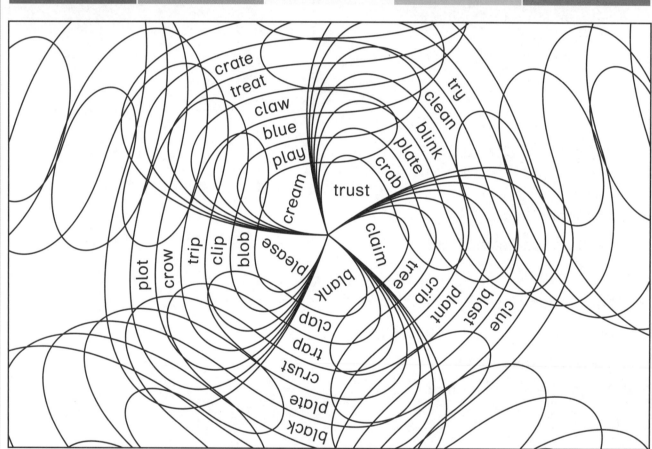

C Listen and spell.

1.		6.	
2.		7.	
3.		8.	
4.		9.	
5.		10.	Score

54

The Toys at Night

I really believe, in the night-time
When I am asleep in my bed,
That my toys get up out of their boxes
And dance on the carpet instead;
For when I get up in the morning,
They're not where I put them at night;
I'm sure that the pistol goes popping –
I'm certain the soldier-toys fight!

The old Noah's Ark in the cupboard
I know goes a-floating away,
Till it reaches a mountain of cushions,,
And there does it settle and stay;
And the animals march out in order –
The lion and leopard and bear:
I wish that I wasn't so sleepy,
For I should so love to be there.

I wish that I wasn't so sleepy,
For then I should stay up and see
The toys that I keep in my cupboard
Go jumping and hopping round me.
Oh! It would be jolly to catch them,
When they thought I was safely in bed;
But as they don't come when you watch them,
I'll imagine them playing instead.

A Answer the questions by filling in the missing words.

soldier-toys   in the cupboard   floats away   in bed   wake up   have fun

1. Where is the child? The child is _____ .

2. What happens at night? The toys _____ at night.

3. Where should the toys be? They should be _____ .

4. Who fights at night? The _____ fight.

5. What happens to Noah's Ark? It _____ at night.

6. What happens in the morning? The children _____ again.

B What do you think?

1. Tick (✓) the boxes. (i) Do you like this poem? Yes ☐ No ☐

   (ii) Do the toys really play at night? Yes ☐ No ☐

2. Name three of your favourite toys.

   (i) _____ (ii) _____ (iii) _____

3. Name two toys that might like to dance at night.

   (i) _____ (ii) _____

4. What two toys might like to escape to the garden?

   (i) _____ (ii) _____

5. Write the line that you like most. _____

C Imagine... Draw a picture of two of your favourite toys.

Unit 18 - Language

A Write sentences. Use the words.

1. toys/night _____
2. ball/carpet _____
3. present/jigsaw _____
4. cushion/behind _____
5. opened/cupboard _____
6. favourite/toy _____

B Tick (✓) the correct boxes.

1.	Jigsaws can be...	soft		angry		interesting		difficult	
2.	Dolls are ...	fun		boring		silly		pretty	
3.	Balls can...	walk		talk		bounce		burst	
4.	Books are...	fun		helpful		interesting		hard	

C All about me!

My favourite toy is _____.

I also have a _____ and a _____.

After school I play with _____.

I keep my toys in the _____. (toybox, playroom, bedroom)

I would love to have a _____.

Draw your favourite game.

56

happy   **happily**   **The baby was happy.**

She played happily with teddy.

A Choose and write.

clear   sad   loud   neat   cheeky   bright
clearly   sadly   loudly   neatly   cheekily   brightly

1. The girl was _____. Her kitten had _____ died.
2. The man shouted _____. He said the music was too _____.
3. His writing was _____. He wrote _____ in the copy.
4. The monkey _____ took the purse. Monkeys can be very _____.
5. The sun shone _____. I love _____ days.
6. The sky is _____. I can _____ see the plane.

B Write and colour. Pick two words to describe each picture.

naughty   shining   walking   happy   sad   shouting
dog   noisily   child   slowly   brightly   baby

shining brightly	_____ _____	_____ _____
_____ _____	_____ _____	_____ _____

C Listen and spell.

1.		6.	
2.		7.	
3.		8.	
4.		9.	
5.		10.	Score

Dogs with jobs

Dogs are lovely pets. They like to play and have fun. They love chasing and playing with a ball. But some dogs do not have time to play because they have jobs. Some dogs work very hard.

The sheepdog helps the farmer. Sheepdogs are usually collie dogs. They have great eyesight, good hearing and a sharp sense of smell. Sheep can wander far away and sometimes end up on dangerous cliffs. The farmer brings his stick and his dog with him to collect the sheep. The dog gathers the sheep and can go far out on a cliff to collect a sheep or lamb. Sheepdogs are quick and clever.

The guide dog helps people with poor eyesight. Guide dogs are usually labrador dogs. They are sensible, caring and clever. They spend time learning at dog school. When they are ready, they are given to somebody who is blind, or almost blind. They are like an extra pair of eyes. They know how to cross the road, avoid dangers, get on buses and collect shopping. Guide dogs are quiet and gentle.

The travel dog helps people in cold, snowy areas. Travel dogs are usually husky dogs. They work as a team with about six or eight dogs in the team. They move quickly on ice and snow. They have a sled (smaller than Santa's). They carry parcels, groceries and people. Travel dogs are strong and sensible.

A Answer the questions.

1. What dog is quiet and gentle? _____
2. What dog is strong and sensible? _____
3. What dog is quick and clever? _____
4. What dog might be...
   (i) on a bus? _____ (ii) in the snow? _____ (iii) on a cliff? _____
5. Which work dog do you think is most important? _____
6. What kind of dog do you like best? _____ Pick a name for a dog. _____

B True (✓) or False (✗)?

1.	Huskies go on buses.		4.	Some dogs do not work.		7.	Huskies can travel far.	
2.	Collies go out on cliffs.		5.	Sheepdogs climb a lot.		8.	Dogs are not good pets.	
3.	Labradors go to school.		6.	Sheepdogs work in teams.		9.	Huskies work in cold weather.	

C Imagine... Draw these dogs. **1.** the hardest worker **2.** your favourite dog

A Write each sentence correctly. Add the missing word.

1. The drives a tractor.
2. The sheepdog helps the.
3. The farmer cuts the wool on the.
4. A is a young sheep.
5. you see the new lambs?
6. I sheep are nice animals.

B Write the words that mean the opposite.

large   hot   ugly   quick   cheap
empty   crying   soft   small   thin

1.	cold		6.	small	
2.	slow		7.	full	
3.	fat		8.	hard	
4.	tall		9.	expensive	
5.	pretty		10.	laughing	

C All about me! Underline one word only.

Sweets can be expensive boring hard.

I prefer the colour pink green yellow.

On my next birthday I will be eight nine ten.

I have a television bookshelf teddy in my bedroom.

I hope I get no easy interesting homework today.

Draw your favourite treat.

A Say the word. Write the sound.

| claw | plant | clown | please | climb | plaster |
| play | clamp | plate | clean | plop | clap |

cl– sound		pl– sound	

B Name and colour. Use the words from Activity A.

_ _ _ _ _ _   _ _ _ _ _ _   _ _ _ _ _

_ _ _ _ _   _ _ _ _ _   _ _ _ _ _ _ _

C Listen and spell.

1.		6.	
2.		7.	
3.		8.	
4.		9.	
5.		10.	

Score

60

Pedro's Gold

Pedro was a rich old man. He had lots of gold but did not want to spend it. Pedro was a miser. He kept his gold in a tin box buried in a hole at the bottom of his garden. Every Friday after supper Pedro would dig up the box to look at his gold. Pedro lived alone. He had neighbours but he did not see them very often. One evening when he went to look at his gold he found the hole dug, the box open and the gold gone!

Pedro cried so loudly that his neighbours came running to see what was wrong. "My money is gone. I am a poor man now," he said. The neighbours tried to console him but he would not listen. "I have nothing left now," he sobbed.

"What did you do with your gold when you had it?" said one neighbour. "I did nothing with it but it made me happy," said Pedro. "Well, do not worry, Pedro," said the neighbour. "Just keep doing what you always did. Close the box and bury it again. Then you can dig it up as usual. Fill it with golden sand and you will have something special in your box."

Pedro laughed. The neighbours laughed. "Thank you very much," he said. "That is exactly what I will do!"

A Answer the questions.

1. Who was Pedro? _____
2. What was in Pedro's box? _____
3. Where was the box kept? _____
4. Why was Pedro sad one day? _____
5. Who came to help Pedro? _____
6. Where did Pedro put the sand? _____

B True (✓) or False (✗)?

Pedro...		The box...		People who have money...	
was young and rich		was in a hole in the garden		never spend it	
kept his gold in a box		was made of wood		are always misers	
had a wooden box		belonged to a neighbour		are not poor	
often visited his neighbours		was made of gold		sometimes save money	

C Imagine... Draw pictures of these. 1. Pedro 2. Pedro's supper

A Write the sentences in the correct order. Draw a picture of one story.

After that I would share the money.

I would buy lots of things.

I wish I had some gold.

1. _____

2. _____

3. _____

I enjoyed them at lunchtime.

I put them in my lunchbox.

Mum made some nice sandwiches.

1. _____

2. _____

3. _____

B Write the correct word.

always   ever   never   sometimes

1. I _____ go out when the sun is shining.

2. Did you _____ get burnt by the sun?

3. You should _____ go out without sun cream.

4. Mum _____ puts cream on me.

5. I _____ put it on myself.

6. I _____ take a little off but I _____ tell her.

7. She would _____ let me out again if I told her.

C What am I?

sunglasses   freckle   swimsuit   cream   sunhat   towel

1. I am a small brown spot on your face. _____

2. I am soft. I go on your face in the sun. _____

3. I am dark. I go on your eyes. _____

4. You wear me in the swimming pool. _____

5. You use me after swimming. _____

What am I?

6. I go on your head to protect you. _____

A Make real words.

–amp   -ale   -oop   -ar   -ip   -ack   -an   -op   -at   -in

t	t	t	t	t
r	r	r	r	r
ch	ch	ch	ch	ch
sc	sc	sc	sc	sc

B Colour by sound.

ole sound	**ale** sound	**eel** sound	**oot** sound	**ay** sound

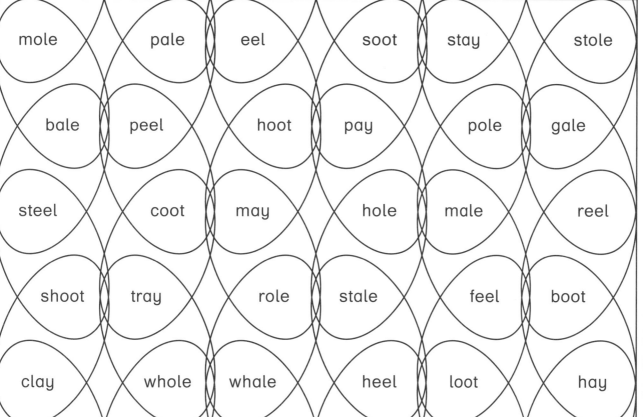

mole   pale   eel   soot   stay   stole

bale   peel   hoot   pay   pole   gale

steel   coot   may   hole   male   reel

shoot   tray   role   stale   feel   boot

clay   whole   whale   heel   loot   hay

C Listen and spell.

I.		6.	
2.		7.	
3.		8.	
4.		9.	
5.		10.	Score

The Caterpillar and the Butterfly

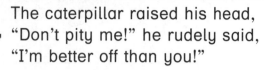

A caterpillar green and fat
Upon a juicy cabbage sat,
Eating all day through;
And when a dazzling butterfly,
Creamy-white, came sailing by,
They both said, "How d'ye do?"

"I hope you like my powdered wings,
They're just the very latest things,"
Said Butterfly, in glee.
"And see my tongue, so long and
    curled,
The finest one in all the world,
A treat for you to see."

"Poor caterpillar! You can't sip
The nectar from a flower's lip,
Nor fly the summer through!"

The caterpillar raised his head,
"Don't pity me!" he rudely said,
"I'm better off than you!"

"I eat all day, I sit and stare,
I want no flying through the air,
I like to creep and crawl.
A butterfly I'd hate to be,
It's best to be a grub like me,
A caterpillar small!"

Then all the elves who listened near
Laughed like anything to hear
The quarrel 'twixt the two;
But neither the grub nor butterfly
Could ever guess, the reason why –
I know it though! Do you?

A Complete the sentences.

cabbage   pretty wings   juicy   young   laughing   green   fly   butterfly   fat

1. The caterpillar is _____ and _____ and likes to eat _____ .
2. The butterfly has _____ and can _____ .
3. The caterpillar sat upon a _____ cabbage.
4. The caterpillar thinks that it is not good to be a _____ .
5. The elves are _____ at the caterpillar and the butterfly.
6. The elves know that a caterpillar is a _____ butterfly.

B What do you think?

1. Do you like the poem? Yes ☐ No ☐ Why? _____
2. Tick (✓) two words that describe the caterpillar.
   pretty ☐   silly ☐   ugly ☐   sad ☐   cross ☐   greedy ☐
3. Tick (✓) two words that describe the butterfly.
   pretty ☐   angry ☐   clever ☐   mean ☐   ugly ☐   cruel ☐
4. Write the line from the poem that you like most. _____

C Imagine... Finish the pictures and colour them.

A Write sentences. Use the words.

1. caterpillar/butterfly   _____
2. sun/dazzling   _____
3. caterpillar/cabbage   _____
4. crawl/leaf   _____
5. butterfly/wings   _____
6. summer/fun   _____

B Tick (✓) the correct boxes.

1.	Caterpillars can...	creep		crawl		fly		dance	
2.	Butterflies can...	swim		fly		sing		dance	
3.	Babies can...	creep		crawl		fly		hop	
4.	I can...	swim		fly		read		write	

C All about me!

I can _____ but I cannot _____ .

I wish I could _____ .

My favourite insect is the _____ .

An insect I am scared of is the _____ .

The insect I see most often is the _____ .

Draw an insect that scares you.

big	bigger	biggest

The sweet is big. The biscuit is bigger.
The cake is the biggest.

A Choose and write.

small   big   funnier   smallest   noisier
funny   smaller   noisy   biggest   scary
noisiest   scarier   bigger   scariest   funniest

1. big: A bicycle is _____. A car is _____. A bus is the _____.
2. noisy: A car is _____. A bus is _____. A plane is the _____.
3. small: A cat is _____. A mouse is _____. A bee is the _____.
4. scary: A dragon is _____. A monster is _____. A ghost is the _____.
5. funny: A story is _____. A joke is _____. A clown is the _____.

B Draw and colour.

a pretty cup	a prettier, bigger cup	the prettiest, biggest cup
a funny, grey cat	a funnier, black cat	the funniest, orange cat

C Listen and spell.

1.		6.	
2.		7.	
3.		8.	
4.		9.	
5.		10.	

Score

Asal on sports day

It was summer. The school sports day was coming. This year there was going to be an extra race – just for ponies. Shay asked if donkeys could be in the race also and the teacher agreed. Maria was worried. After all Asal was a donkey. Everybody knows that ponies run much faster than donkeys.

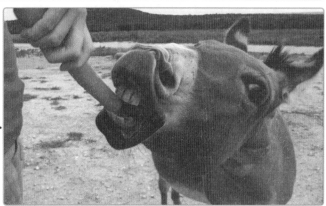

Each day after school Maria brought Asal to the beach to practise. Asal worked hard and was good, but the ponies were all bigger and faster.

Grandad Leo heard about the problem. He knew Asal loved carrots. He thought of a plan. On sports day all the big ponies were in a line ready to run. Little Asal was there too but Shay and Maria could not believe their eyes. There was a carrot tied to a stick in front of Asal's nose. Grandad knew that Asal would run fast to try to catch the carrot.

The teacher blew the whistle. The big ponies were all very quick, but Asal was much quicker. Asal kept running to try to catch the carrot. Asal won the race! Everybody cheered. The teacher gave Asal a medal. Shay took the carrot off the stick and gave it to Asal. Maria ran to Grandad Leo and gave him a big hug. Grandad Leo winked and smiled.

A   Answer the questions by filling in the missing words.

> a medal   The ponies   The sports day
> Grandad Leo   ponies and donkeys   a carrot

1. What was happening soon at school? _____ was happening soon.
2. What was the special race? The special race was a race for _____ .
3. Who did Maria think would be too quick? _____ would be too quick.
4. Who thought of a plan? _____ thought of a plan.
5. What did Grandad Leo put in front of Asal? He put _____ in front of Asal.
6. What prize did Asal get? Asal got _____ .

B   True (✓) or False (✗)?

1.	Asal was a small pony.		4.	The teacher won the race.		7.	Grandad Leo won a medal.	
2.	Ponies are good at running.		5.	Grandad Leo had a plan.		8.	Asal came last in the race.	
3.	Maria was worried about Asal.		6.	Maria and Shay cheated.		9.	Asal won a medal.	

C   Imagine... You have a camera. Show the photos you have of these:

1. Asal's medal   2. Grandad Leo winking   3. Maria and Shay

A   Write words that end with the same sound.

1.	–ay	hay	
2.	–am		
3.	–all		
4.	–are		
5.	–ate		

B   Write three sentences about the story.

farmer   dog   chicken   running   tractor   laughing   tractor   grunting

1. _____

2. _____

3. _____

C   Write the sentences correctly.

1. got the I meat shop. in the   _____

2. you money? got Have some   _____

3. bag. give Please my me own   _____

4. no I today. homework got   _____

5. tasted The nice. very cake   _____

STOP AND LEARN!   NOUNS   A noun is a person, a place or a thing.
Example: A donkey is an animal that lives on a farm.

A Ring the nouns.

duck	running	horse	town	John	table
very	teacher	boat	happy	small	man
crisps	always	flower	Dublin	afraid	homework
school	shoes	sister	heavy	computer	Michelle
coat	bag	hungry	father	climbing	school

B Finish the sentences by adding nouns.

1. The _____ bought a _____ in the _____ .
2. I see _____ eating _____ in the _____ .
3. _____ gave me a _____ from the _____ .
4. I look at _____ on the _____ every _____ .
5. I have _____ in my _____ for _____ .

Draw a picture that has three nouns in it.

C Listen and spell.

1.		6.	
2.		7.	
3.		8.	
4.		9.	
5.		10.	

Score

The Saggy Baggy Elephant

Sooki was a baby elephant. He did not know that he was an elephant. He was lost. He saw a parrot laughing at him. "Your skin does not fit," said the parrot. "You are a saggy baggy elephant!"

Poor Sooki! He looked. He saw lots of wrinkles. He tried to fix the wrinkles with his trunk but it was no good. He pulled up the skin on his legs but it fell back down again.

Sooki saw a tiger. "Tiger, please tell me why your skin fits so well," said Sooki. "I run and jump all the time," said the tiger. "I keep fit. That is why I have beautiful skin." Sooki ran and jumped. He hopped on one leg. He even did some press-ups but it was no good. Sooki was tired and thirsty. He went to the water to get a drink. He saw the parrot again. "Go into the water," said the parrot. "Maybe your skin will shrink." Sooki went into the water but a crocodile came and tried to nibble his ears. Poor Sooki was lonely and sad. "I will hide in the dark and nobody will laugh at me," said Sooki. Sooki went into a cave. "Nobody will see my saggy baggy skin now," he said.

Suddenly Sooki heard a lot of crashing and stamping. He peeped out. He saw lots of big, grey, wrinkled animals just like himself. "Look at those beautiful animals!" said Sooki.

The elephants smiled at Sooki. "I wish I looked just like you," said Sooki. "You do!" said the elephants. "You are a beautiful baby elephant. Come and join us."

A **Answer the questions.**

1. Who was Sooki? _____
2. What was the parrot doing? _____
3. What was wrong with Sooki's skin? _____
4. Who did Sooki see next? _____
5. What animal was in the water? _____
6. Where did Sooki hide? _____

B **True (✓) or False (✗)?**

Sooki...		Elephants...		The story...	
was an elephant		are small animals		I like the story.	
was very happy		have big ears		I like the parrot.	
liked his skin		have no friends		I like the tiger.	
hid in the water		have trunks		I like Sooki.	
saw more beautiful elephants		have lots of wrinkles		I think the story is sad.	

C **Imagine... Draw pictures of these.** **1.** Sooki **2.** the parrot **3.** the tiger

A **Write the story correctly.**

The children were at school.

They ran out into the field.

The teacher said it was sports day.

Soon the races began.

They were very excited.

The children put on their tracksuits.

1. _____

2. _____

3. _____

4. _____

5. _____

6. _____

B **Write the correct word.**

given   give   gave

1. The teacher _____ me homework.

2. She does not _____ homework every day.

3. Last year I was always _____ homework.

4. Mum _____ me a note for the teacher.

5. She said the teacher had _____ me too much homework.

6. I forgot to _____ the teacher the note.

7. I wish I had _____ it to her but I will _____ it to her tomorrow.

C **What am I?**

homework   note   bell   schoolbag   lunchbox   pencil case

1. It is smaller than a schoolbag. There is food in it. _____

2. I gave it to the teacher. The teacher read it. _____

3. It makes noise. I hear it in the morning. _____

4. It is smaller than a schoolbag. I have a pencil in it. _____

5. The teacher gave it to me. Sometimes it is hard to do. _____

6. I bring it to school every day. I put my books in it. _____

A Make real words.

st–   cr–   sh–   th–   gr–   br–   pl–   sm–   fl–   sp–   cl–   dr–   sl–

____ate	____ate	____ate	____ate	____ate
____ave	____ave	____ave	____ave	____ave
____ank	____ank	____ank	____ank	____ank
____ash	____ash	____ash	____ash	____ash

B Write three sentences about the story.

elephant   monkey   crying   cross

ice-cream   laughing   splashing   embarrassed

I. _____

2. _____

3. _____

C Listen and spell.

1.		6.	
2.		7.	
3.		8.	
4.		9.	
5.		10.	

Score [   ]

My Dog

Have you seen a little dog,
Anywhere about?
A raggy dog, a shaggy dog
who is always looking out
for some fresh mischief
which he thinks he ought to do,
He's very likely, at this minute,
biting someone's shoe.

If you see that little dog,
his tail up in the air,
A whirly tail, a curly tail,
a dog who does not care
For any other dog he meets,
not even for himself,
Then hide your mats
and put your meat upon the shelf.

If you see that little dog,
barking at the cars,
A raggy dog, a shaggy dog,
with eyes like twinkling stars,
Just let me know
for though he's bad as bad can be,
I wouldn't change that dog
for all the treasures of the sea!

A Answer the questions by filling in the missing words.

raggy   lost   shaggy   whirly   twinkling stars   barks   bites   curly

1. What is wrong? A dog is _____ .
2. Write two words that describe the dog. He is _____ and _____ .
3. What kind of tail has he got? He has a _____ , _____ tail.
4. What kind of eyes has he got? He has eyes like _____ .
5. What does he do with people's shoes? He _____ the shoes.
6. What does he do when he sees cars? He _____ at the cars.

B What do you think?

1. Do you like the poem? Yes ☐ No ☐ Why? I think it is a _____ poem.
2. Tick (✓) two words that describe the dog.
   lonely ☐   bold ☐   clever ☐   untidy ☐   silly ☐   scared ☐
3. Tick (✓) two words that describe the owner.
   delighted ☐   worried ☐   careless ☐   kind ☐   cruel ☐
4. Do you have a dog? Yes ☐ No ☐ Pick a nice name for a dog. _____

C Imagine...
Draw a picture of an unusual-looking dog.

A Write sentences. Use the words.

1. dog/bite _____
2. bone/butcher _____
3. friend/pet _____
4. curly/shaggy _____
5. barking/cars _____
6. tail/little _____

B Tick (✓) the correct boxes.

1.	Dogs are...	friendly		helpful		sneaky		useless	
2.	Dogs can...	bite		bake		bark		burst	
3.	Dogs I like are...	gentle		scary		untidy		crazy	
4.	I would love a...	horse		dog		hamster		monkey	

C All about me!

In the zoo I like _____ and _____ .

On the farm I like _____ and _____ .

My favourite pets are _____ and _____ .

I think the scariest pet would be a _____ .

I would not feed my pet _____ and _____ .

Draw two foods for dogs.

long   **longer**   **longest**

A day is long. **A week is** longer.
A month is longest.

A Choose and write.

longer   wilder   angry   greatest   shortest
short   great   longest   angriest   greater
angrier   wildest   wild   shorter   long

1. long: a _____ stick   a _____ stick   the _____ stick
2. angry: an _____ lion   an _____ lion   the _____ lion
3. great: a _____ meal   a _____ meal   the _____ meal
4. short: a _____ story   a _____ story   the _____ story
5. wild: a _____ child   a _____ child   the _____ child

B Draw and colour.

an unhappy dog	an unhappier dog	the unhappiest dog
an old, green book	an older, brown book	the oldest, red book

C Listen and spell.

1.		6.	
2.		7.	
3.		8.	
4.		9.	
5.		10.	

Score

75

The Fox in the Well

The fox is a clever animal. He can play tricks on others. When people do something smart we say they are "as cute as a fox".

Foxes sleep during the day and look for food at night. One night long ago, a fox was very hungry. The full moon was shining brightly, but the fox could find no food. He passed by a water well. The reflection of the moon shone like a bright yellow circle in the water at the bottom of the well. The fox thought the moon was a circle of yellow cheese. He jumped into the bucket in the well and went to the bottom.

There was no cheese at the bottom – just the moon's reflection The fox was now trapped. He could not leave the well until another person or animal came down in the second bucket. He waited two days. He was cold, lonely and very hungry.

On the third day a wolf passed the well. He stopped and looked down. He saw the fox. "Oh, Mr Wolf, I have the most delicious cheese down here. Do come and join me," said the fox.

The foolish wolf jumped into the second bucket. As the wolf went down the fox was able to go back up to the top of the well in his bucket. The wolf shouted for help but the clever fox had run away.

A   Answer the questions.

1. Why was the fox out at night? _____
2. Tick (✓)the boxes. Was the fox…
   (i) thirsty? Yes ☐ No ☐ (ii) hungry? Yes ☐ No ☐ (iii) sleepy? Yes ☐ No ☐
3. What did the fox think was in the well? _____
4. What was really there? _____
5. Was the wolf clever? _____

B   True (✓) or False (✗)?

About the fox...		About the wolf...	
The fox hunts for food at night.		The wolf looks a bit like a dog.	
The fox lives as a pet in the house.		The wolf is gentle and kind.	
The fox eats chickens and rabbits.		The wolf lives in woods and caves.	
The fox has a bushy tail.		The wolf is not as clever as the fox.	
The fox sleeps during the night.		The wolf wanted cheese.	

C   Imagine… Draw pictures of these.

1. the cheese in the well   2. the moon in the sky   3. the fox in the bucket

STOP AND LEARN! ADJECTIVES Adjectives **tell more about** nouns.
Example: The little **boy had a** big **train.**
REMEMBER **A** noun **is a** person, **a place or a** thing.

A Ring the adjectives.

pretty	boy	greedy	fell	baby	old
soft	angry	coat	happy	small	playing
amazing	in	flower	scary	school	jumped
teacher	sunny	ran	heavy	computer	crazy
coat	bag	hungry	father	climbing	school

B Select the best adjectives for each sentence.

red nasty funny enormous big frightened fluffy good kind
forgetful beautiful hungry yellow green old little tasty happy

1. The _____ lady left her _____ bag in the library.

2. Jimmy bought a _____ toy in the _____ shop.

3. The _____ elephant splashed the _____ child in the zoo.

4. The _____ clown jumped over the _____ ball in the circus.

5. Matty crashed his _____ car into the _____ lorry.

6. The _____ teacher had a _____ box of sweets on his desk.

7. Santa gave the _____ child a _____ present.

8. After school the _____ children played in the _____ garden.

9. Amy bought a _____ meal for her _____ granny.

10. I would love a _____ _____ puppy.

C Write each sentence correctly.

1. the the old I table. book put on   *I put the old book on the table.*

2. give flower. me the Please pretty   _____

3. want I a hat. funny big   _____

4. old was working. television The not   _____

5. dog? you see old the Can grumpy   _____

A Write words that begin with the same sound.

sh	share	sh_____	sh_____
ch	ch_____	ch_____	ch_____
tr	tr_____	tr_____	tr_____
br	br_____	br_____	br_____
fl	fl_____	fl_____	fl_____

B Write three sentences about the story.

sailing   blowing   wind   dolphin   jumping   laughing   throwing   stick

1. _____

2. _____

3. _____

C Listen and spell.

1.		6.	
2.		7.	
3.		8.	
4.		9.	
5.		10.	

Score

Ducks in danger

Baby ducks, called ducklings, are born in a nest. The nest is often built in long grass beside a river. The mother lays between six and eight eggs. She spends some weeks sitting on the eggs to keep them warm. She sometimes leaves to get some food but soon returns. She is a good mother. One day the eggs begin to crack open. The ducklings are now ready to come out

of the shells. This is called hatching. The mother keeps them warm, feeds them and teaches them how to behave. She helps them to walk, to swim, to get food and to avoid danger. Baby ducks are good at following their mother everywhere. They stay close by at all times. Other animals, like the fox, are waiting to snap up a baby duck for dinner. Even greedy birds might eat them.

One day a mother duck was teaching her eight babies to swim in Saint Stephen's Green in Dublin. A cheeky seagull swooped down and grabbed a duckling. Mother duck was very upset because her baby was gone. The other ducks were scared. Suddenly the greedy seagull came back! He grabbed another baby duck but this time mother duck was ready. "Quack, quack, quack," she screeched. A fight began, with lots of quacking and flapping. Mother duck was very angry. The seagull was frightened and dropped the little duckling. Mother duck put him under her wing to mind him.

A Answer the questions by filling in the missing words.

    hatched   nest   swim   mother   seagull   duckling   fox

1. Where are baby ducks born? They are born in a _____.
2. Who keeps the eggs warm? The _____ keeps them warm.
3. What happens when the shells crack? The ducklings are _____.
4. What does the mother teach her ducklings? She teaches them to _____.
5. Name two animals that might eat baby ducks. (i) _____ (ii) _____
6. What is a baby duck called? A baby duck is called a _____.

B True (✓) or False (✗)?

1.	Mother ducks are good.		4.	Baby ducks learn to read.		7.	The mother duck was delighted.	
2.	Ducklings hatch out of eggs.		5.	Baby ducks learn to swim.		8.	The seagull came back again.	
3.	Foxes like to eat ducks.		6.	A greedy seagull stole a duckling.		9.	The mother had a big fight.	

C Imagine... Draw a picture of the ducklings learning to swim.

A Write the story correctly.

Suddenly a greedy seagull arrived.
The children were walking in the park.
The seagull grabbed a baby duck.
They saw Mother Duck on the water.
Mother Duck flew after the seagull.
Mother Duck had five baby ducks.

1. _____

2. _____

3. _____

4. _____

5. _____

6. _____

B Write the correct word.

will   when   what   which

1. Mother Duck _____ always mind her babies.

2. They are very small _____ they are born.

3. It is hard to know _____ baby is the cutest.

4. Mother Duck knows _____ her babies need.

5. Ducks stay near their mother _____ they are small.

6. _____ they are bigger they _____ learn to swim.

7. Ducklings should do _____ Mother Duck says.

C What am I?

feathers   water   wings   duckling   nest   eggs

1. A duck has two of these.   _____

2. These are in the nest.   _____

3. It is wet. Ducks swim in it.   _____

4. This is a baby duck.   _____

5. Ducks make this. They put the eggs in it.   _____

6. They are soft. Birds have lots of them.   _____

A Make real words.

st–	sm–	sh–	th–	gr–
br–	bl–	sm–	fl–	sp–
s–	w–	t–	h–	f–	m–

___ing	___ing	___ing	___ing	___ing
___are	___are	___are	___are	___are
___all	___all	___all	___all	___all
___ate	___ate	___ate	___ate	___ate

B Write three sentences about the story.

duckling	umbrella	sunny	ball	water
happy	Mother Duck	pond	straying	

1. _____ .

2. _____ .

3. _____ .

C Listen and spell.

1.		6.	
2.		7.	
3.		8.	
4.		9.	
5.		10.	

Score

Today I Had a Rotten Day

Today I had a rotten day.
As I was coming in from play
I accidentally stubbed my toes
and tripped and fell and whacked my
    nose.

I banged my elbow, barked my shin.
A welt is forming on my chin.
My pencil poked me in the thigh.
I got an eyelash in my eye.

I chipped a tooth. I cut my lip.
I scraped my knee. I hurt my hip.
I pulled my shoulder, tweaked my ear,
and got a bruise upon my rear.

I sprained my back. I wrenched my
    neck.
I'm feeling like a total wreck.
So that's the last time I refuse
when teacher says to tie my shoes.

A **Complete the sentences.**

whacked   rear   His pencil   An eyelash   his shoes

1. He _____ his nose.
2. _____ poked him in the thigh.
3. _____ was in his eye.
4. The teacher told him to tie _____.
5. He got a bruise upon his _____.

B **What do you think?**

1. Tick (✓) the boxes. Is the poem...
   (i) funny? Yes ☐ No ☐ (ii) ridiculous? Yes ☐ No ☐ (iii) clever? Yes ☐ No ☐
2. Tick (✓) two words that tell what this person is like.
   careless ☐   silly ☐   unlucky ☐   brave ☐   naughty ☐   clumsy ☐
3. Tick (✓) two words that tell how you feel when you fall.
   sore ☐   angry ☐   embarrassed ☐   silly ☐   delighted ☐   upset ☐
4. Write the line that you like most. _____
5. Does your mum give you a treat when you fall? _____

C **Imagine... Draw pictures of these.**

1. a sore knee	2. a bandage	3. an open shoelace

A Write sentences. Use the words.

1. today/teeth   _____
2. sprained/ankle   _____
3. nose/bruised   _____
4. pencil/sharp   _____
5. shoes/tie   _____
6. refused/homework   _____

B Tick (✓) the correct boxes.

1.	My eyes are...	sparkly		scary		green		brown	
2.	I once hurt my...	nose		shoulder		ankle		finger	
3.	I have a nice...	smile		face		hand		chin	
4.	Shoes can have...	laces		hair		bows		straps	

C All about me!

Once I fell in the _____.

I hurt my _____ and my _____.

_____ came to help me.

_____ gave me a _____.

I was _____ after a while. (sore, tired, happy, delighted)

Draw yourself falling.

A Write three words for each.

1. animals that like water   _duck_   _fish_   _hippopotamus_
2. things on your face
3. things you eat
4. things in your schoolbag
5. things that are hot
6. things that are scary

B Crack the code.

Ω	¥	÷	§	₪	≥	∞	●	→	#	Δ	♥	☺	◊
a	c	d	e	h	I	i	k	l	o	r	s	t	w

≥
I

→	∞	●	§
l	i	k	e

♥	¥	₪	#	#	→
s	c	h	o	o	l

≥

→	∞	●	§

☺	#

Δ	§	Ω	÷

≥

→	∞	●	§

☺	#

◊	Δ	∞	☺	§

Draw yourself having a good day.

C Listen and spell.

1.		6.	
2.		7.	
3.		8.	
4.		9.	
5.		10.	

Score

The Cat and the Bell

Once upon a time an old lady lived in a very old house. There were lots of mice in the house. The lady was not happy with the mice. They ate her cheese. They ate her meat. They ate her biscuits. They made noise at night and she could not sleep. "I must get a cat," she said. So she got a cat and the cat killed lots of mice. The lady was happy and the cat was happy too. But the mice were not happy. Indeed they were very unhappy!

The oldest mouse said, "All mice must come to my hole tonight. We will have a meeting. We must think what we can do about the cat."

All the mice came to the meeting. Many of the mice spoke at the meeting but they did not know what to do. At last one of the young mice spoke. "We must put a bell on the cat," he said. "When the cat is coming we shall hear the bell and we can run and hide. The cat will not catch any more mice!"

Then an old mouse spoke. "Who will put the bell on the cat?" he said. No mouse answered. He waited and still no mouse answered. At last the old mouse spoke again. He said, "It is not hard to say things, but it is much harder to do them."

A Complete the sentences.

1. An old _____ lived in a very old _____ .
2. There were _____ in the _____ lady's house .
3. The lady was not _____ so she got a _____ .
4. The mice were very _____ so they called a _____ .
5. A young _____ said, "We must put a _____ on the cat."

B True (✓) or False (✗)?

About the story...		About you...	
The old lady had a dog.		I have a cat at home.	
There were mice in the house.		I have a dog at home.	
The cat likes to catch mice.		I think mice are rather nice.	
The old lady put a bell on the cat.		I would like a new pet.	
The old mouse put a bell on the cat.		I think my teacher does not like mice.	

C Imagine... Draw pictures of these. **1.** the old lady **2.** the cat

A Write the story correctly.

The mice decided on a plan.
However the mice were scared and ran away.
The cat liked to eat mice.
The little mouse got a nice big bell.
Soon they saw the cat coming.
The mice all waited quietly.

1. _____

2. _____

3. _____

4. _____

5. _____

6. _____

B Write the correct word.

did   done   does

1. I have _____ my homework. I _____ it after school.

2. _____ your dad know what you have _____?

3. The boy had _____ the cleaning.

4. Mum said she _____ not know who _____ it.

5. Tom said he had not _____ it, but I think he _____ it.

6. _____ you forget to tell who _____ it?

C What am I?

flower   vegetable   clay   grass   tree   fruit

1. I am colourful. I am quite sweet to eat.   _____

2. I am large. I grow. You can climb on me.   _____

3. I grow. I am tasty. You cook me.   _____

4. I grow. You can cut me but only animals eat me.   _____

5. I am dark. I can be mucky when it is wet.   _____

6. I am colourful. I look nice in a vase.   _____

A Write three words for each.

1. things you like   _television_   _my friend_   _spaghetti_
2. programmes you watch on television _____
3. things you do in the garden _____
4. things you don't like _____
5. things that are heavy _____
6. things you find in the bedroom _____

B Crack the code.

Ω	¥	⌂	÷	§	€	Π	₪	≥	∞	●	→	≠	☺	#	Σ	△	♥	☻	◊	∩	√
a	c	C	d	e	f	g	h	I	i	k	l	m	M	n	o	r	s	t	u	v	w

☺	∞	¥	§
M	i	c	e

₪	Ω	∩	§

→	Σ	#	Π

☻	Ω	∞	→	♥

⌂	Ω	☻	♥

₪	Ω	∩	§

√	₪	∞	♥	●	§	△	♥

☺	∞	¥	§

÷	Σ

#	Σ	☻

→	∞	●	§

¥	Ω	☻	♥

C Listen and spell.

1.		6.	
2.		7.	
3.		8.	
4.		9.	
5.		10.	Score

The Bee and the Spider

A bee buzzed around the flowers in a garden. "Keep away, you silly thing!" said an angry voice. It was a spider. He had just finished making a web. "Keep away!" he said again. "I do not want you breaking my nice new web," he said. "Good morning," said the bee. "How did you make such a nice web?" The spider was pleased.

"I make long threads first. I shape them like the spokes of a wheel. I fasten the ends to a twig or leaf. Then I weave more threads round and round the spokes. I put little drops of gluey juice where the threads cross. It looks nice but it is a trap. It is a fly trap. The glue sticks to the legs of the flies and they cannot escape. Then I eat them for dinner."

"You are such a clever insect," said the bee. "I am not an insect," said the spider. "Insects have three parts in their bodies. I only have two and I am much more important. I also have eight eyes. They do not move but they help me to organise the threads for my web."

"Very interesting," said the bee, "but I make honey that is good for people. I carry pollen from flower to flower. That helps plants to make seeds."

"Huh! I suppose that is important," said the spider. "But I kill flies. Flies can be dirty. They can get into fruit like apples and destroy them."

"I see," said the humble bee. "We both do good work. Excuse me now. I must fly home and empty my honey bags. Bzz-bye!"

A Answer the questions by filling in the missing words.

the flowers   web   spider   spreads pollen   bee   traps flies

1. Who was in the garden? A _____ and a _____ were in the garden.
2. What was the spider making? He was making a _____.
3. Where was the bee buzzing? She was buzzing around _____.
4. Name something that the spider does. The spider _____.
5. Name something that the bee does. The bee _____.
6. Which do you prefer – the spider or the bee? I prefer the _____.

B True (✓) or False (✗)?

1.	Bees can sting you.		5.	Spiders collect honey.	
2.	Bees can make webs.		6.	Spiders make webs.	
3.	Bees can trap flies.		7.	Spiders have eight eyes.	
4.	Bees like flowers.		8.	Spiders are insects.	

C Imagine… Unscramble the words. Draw a picture of each one.

1. bew _____   2. owrfle _____   3. nyohe _____

STOP AND LEARN! **VERBS** Verbs **are** actions. **Things** happen **with** verbs.
Example: **The boy** screamed **and** ran **away.**

A Ring the verbs.

running	feather	greedy	fell	chased	took
boots	cutting	camera	brought	waiting	playing
worker	found	grass	tired	made	jumped
doctor	sunny	giving	swimming	book	gentle

B Select the best verbs for each sentence.

got crashed chewed hugged jumped put wore cooked drove
played ate corrected cooked brought went broke crashed kicked

1. I _____ Mum this morning.
2. Sophie _____ a meal for her granny.
3. The goat _____ the grass and then _____ the fence.
4. Jimmy _____ a ball and _____ in the garden.
5. Did you _____ the lunch on the table?
6. Molly _____ the new jumper at school.
7. Jamie _____ his car and then _____ it in the garage.
8. The teacher _____ the homework.
9. Santa _____ presents and _____ them under the tree.
10. I _____ in the park and then I _____ home.

C Write each sentence correctly.

1. will friend My today. with play me   *My friend will play with me today.*
2. football I to play love in field. the   _____
3. dinner The I most spaghetti. is like   _____
4. put on Please coat your hat. and   _____
5. turn It time is television. off the to   _____
6. make webs Spiders catch flies to.   _____

A   Write words that begin with the same sound.

bl	bl_____	bl_____	bl_____
cl	cl_____	cl_____	cl_____
sn	sn_____	sn_____	sn_____
dr	dr_____	dr_____	dr_____
pl	pl_____	pl_____	pl_____

B   Write three sentences about the story.

buzzing   reading   chair   climbing   garden   sunny   flowers   tree

1. _____

2. _____

3. _____

C   Listen and spell.

1.		6.	
2.		7.	
3.		8.	
4.		9.	
5.		10.	Score

Sea creatures

Undersea

Beneath the waters
green and cool
The mermaids keep
A swimming school.

The oysters trot;
the lobsters prance;
The dolphins come
To join the dance.

But the jellyfish
who are rather small
Can't seem to learn
The steps at all.

Shark

I went to the aquarium,
And in a tank so dark,
I saw a smooth and swimmy shape,
And knew it was a shark.

I went to the aquarium,
And through a wall of glass,
I saw that shark and thought –
Oh! What a lot of teeth he has!

He swam around so quietly,
He swam around so quick –
I'm awfully glad,
That his tank had
That wall of glass, so thick!

A Answer the questions.

1. Who had (i) a swimming school? _____ (ii) lots of teeth? _____
2. Who (i) trots? _____ (ii) prances? _____
   (iii) can't dance at all? _____
3. Which poem do you like more? _____ Why? _____ .
4. Find words in the poems that sound like:
   (i) bank _____   (ii) chance _____   (iii) pool _____
   (iv) sick _____   (v) tall _____   (vi) pass _____

B What do you think?

1. Do you think fish really dance underwater? Yes ☐ No ☐
2. Tick (✓) the words that are names of fish.
   cod ☐   caterpillar ☐   salmon ☐   crab ☐   ladybird ☐   spider ☐
3. Do you like to eat fish? Yes ☐ No ☐ What is nice to eat with fish? _____
4. What is your favourite dinner? I really like _____ for dinner.
5. What dinner do you not like to eat? I do not like _____ for dinner.
6. Write three foods that are healthy to eat.
   (i) _____   (ii) _____   (iii) _____

C Imagine… Draw a picture of the fish in swimming school.

A Write sentences. Use the words.

1. swimming/school _____
2. fish/swimmers _____
3. dancing/steps _____
4. glass/tank _____
5. shape/funny _____
6. large/fish _____

B Tick (✓) the correct boxes.

1.	Dolphins are...	large		friendly		wobbly		clever	
2.	Jellyfish are...	soft		bony		huge		wobbly	
3.	Lobsters have...	shoes		shells		ships		shores	
4.	Dentists are...	scary		helpful		strong		clever	

C All about me!

I _____ like to eat fish. (do, do not)

I think the _____ is a funny fish.

The fish I would not like to meet is a _____.

Most fish have lots of _____. (bones, beans, branches)

If I had a pet fish it would be a _____.

Draw a fish.

A Write three words for each.

1. types of fish   salmon   shark   cod
2. things you see in the garden
3. things you do at school
4. things you find at the seaside
5. things that are cold
6. things you find in the bathroom

B Crack the code.

Ω	¥	÷	§	⌂	Π	₪	≥	∞	●	→	†	#	Σ	Δ	♥	☻	☺	◊	≈
a	c	d	e	f	g	h	I	i	k	l	m	n	o	r	s	t	T	u	w

☺ ₪ § → **The**

♥ § Ω ♥ ∞ ÷ § → **seaside**

∞ ♥ → **is**

⌂ ◊ # → **fun**

≥ → **I**

→ ∞ ● § → **like**

☺ Σ → **To**

Π Σ → **go**

♥ ≈ ∞ † † ∞ # Π → **swimming**

≥ → **I**

† Ω ● § → **make**

♥ Ω # ÷ ¥ Ω ♥ ☻ → → § ♥ → **sandcastles**

☺ Σ Σ → **too**

C Listen and spell.

1.		6.	
2.		7.	
3.		8.	
4.		9.	
5.		10.	

Score

1 –y	2 –ick	3 –ear	4 –ank	5 –ark	6 –amp
by	lick	ear	bank	bark	camp
my	pick	bear	rank	dark	damp
cry	sick	fear	tank	lark	lamp
fly	tick	hear	sank	mark	ramp
fry	brick	gear	drank	park	champ
shy	chick	near	flank	shark	clamp
sky	flick	pear	plank	spark	cramp
sty	quick	tear	prank	stark	scamp
try	stick	wear	stank	remark	stamp
why	trick	clear	thank	skylark	tramp

7 –oat	8 –ty	9 –ight	10 –oon	11 –ance	12 –een
coat	batty	fight	moon	dance	been
boat	chatty	light	noon	chance	seen
goat	dusty	might	soon	glance	green
moat	empty	night	spoon	France	queen
bloat	frosty	right	baboon	prance	sheen
float	nasty	sight	balloon	advance	between
gloat	nutty	tight	cartoon	balance	sixteen
stoat	party	bright	afternoon	distance	thirteen
throat	scatty	fright	teaspoon	entrance	sunscreen
raincoat	tasty	delight	tablespoon	importance	evergreen

13 –ape	14 –ant	15 –atch	16 –ice	17 st–	18 th–
ape	want	batch	ice	stall	than
cape	giant	catch	mice	stand	that
escape	grant	hatch	nice	start	them
gape	plant	latch	rice	stay	there
grape	infant	match	juice	stick	these
tape	brilliant	patch	voice	still	they
shape	elegant	watch	slice	stole	think
reshape	elephant	snatch	twice	stool	this
landscape	pleasant	unlatch	choice	stop	those
seascape	servant	rematch	office	stuck	three

19 wh–	20 –air	21 –ink	22 –ck	23 –ove	24 –ow
wheel	air	blink	back	cove	grow
when	chair	clink	neck	dove	slow
where	hair	drink	black	love	snow
which	pair	pink	brick	above	throw
whisk	repair	sink	clock	glove	below
whisper	fair	slink	knock	prove	follow
whistle	funfair	stink	quick	shove	shadow
white	unfair	think	shock	stove	window
who	armchair	wink	track	approve	yellow
why	wheelchair	rethink	attack	disapprove	tomorrow

25 –ing	26 –ing	27 –ing	28 –ing	29 –ing	30 ex–
king	calling	dipping	baking	bashing	exact
ring	falling	hopping	caring	lashing	extra
sing	filling	getting	coming	mashing	excite
wing	pulling	letting	having	walking	expect
bring	selling	tipping	taking	washing	exactly
sting	telling	running	blaming	clashing	examine
thing	willing	wagging	leaving	crashing	example
swing	chilling	flipping	scaring	smashing	explain
spring	smelling	dropping	sharing	squashing	exciting
everything	swelling	shopping	shaking	stashing	exercise

Home	People	Body	Clothes	Weather
attic	mother	arms	coat	blustery
bathroom	father	ears	gloves	breezy
bedroom	brother	eyes	jumper	chilly
dining room	sister	face	scarf	foggy
garage	grandmother	fingers	shirt	frosty
garden	grandfather	head	shoes	misty
house	friend	legs	skirt	rainy
kitchen	teacher	nose	tie	stormy
living room	principal	tongue	trousers	sunny
playroom	children	tummy	uniform	windy

School	Playground	Town	Country	Travel
answer	bullying	baker	animals	aeroplane
friends	chasing	butcher	countryside	arrived
homework	dangerous	enjoying	cousins	bicycle
learning	fighting	park	farmer	motorcar
mathematics	football	pond	farmyard	passenger
question	football pitch	shopping	fields	sandwich
reading	goalposts	shops	market	station
schoolbag	playing	supermarket	seaside	ticket
singing	skipping	trolley	tractor	train
writing	weather	walking	visiting	travelling

Months	Days	Time	Birds	Animals
September	Monday	morning	blackbird	bear
October	Tuesday	evening	bluetit	cat
November	Wednesday	afternoon	crow	cow
December	Thursday	daytime	lark	dog
January	Friday	night-time	magpie	elephant
February	Saturday	early	owl	fox
March	Sunday	hour	robin	goat
April	yesterday	minute	seagull	horse
May	today	o'clock	sparrow	mouse
June	tomorrow	half past	starling	rabbit
July	weekdays	quarter past	thrush	sheep
August	weekend	quarter to	wren	wolf

Food	Fruit	Vegetables	Electrics	Moods
breakfast	apple	beans	computer	anxious
lunch	apricot	broccoli	gadget	grumpy
dinner	grapes	cabbage	internet	happy
lunchbox	orange	carrots	laptop	jolly
drink	peach	cauliflower	message	jumpy
sandwich	pear	celery	mobile phone	moody
yoghurt	pineapple	leeks	power	nervous
potatoes	plum	parsnip	printer	noisy
vegetable	raspberry	peas	remote control	quiet
dessert	strawberry	potatoes	television	tired

SPELL-WELL HINTS

1. Look carefully	3. Sound aloud	5. Write and check	7. Check again
2. Spot the pattern	4. Learn aloud	6. Learn again	8. Write again

REMEMBER If adding -ing to one-syllable words ending in a vowel – drop the vowel. | bake – baking

A STORY IN A SENTENCE

1. Think about your story.		2. Write your story.								3. Draw a picture of your story. Have Fun!
I watched	*Grandad's*	*delightful,*	*nutty,*	*old*	*dragon*	*gobbling*	*the teacher's*	*delicious,*	*juicy*	*lunch.*
1. I saw	the	amusing,	friendly,	old	baby	eating	the	puzzled,	old	puppy.
2. I heard	my	angry,	grumpy,		cat	hiding	a	tired,	heavy	snake.
3. I helped	Mum's	anxious,	heavy,	silly	child	gobbling	some	small,	fat	elephant.
4. I did not see	Dad's	big,	jealous,	sleepy	cousin	chasing	one	squeaky,	old	teacher.
5. I watched	our	bitter,	jumpy,	small	dog	squashing	our	grumpy,	crinkly	car.
6. At home	Grandad's	brutal,	nasty,	squeaky	dragon	played with	my	heavy,	big	toy.
7. In the shop	Mam's	bubbly,	nutty,	tall	magician	bought	Dad's	skinny,	orange	computer.
8. At the zoo	your	crinkly,	old,	teeny	teacher	chewed	your	bumpy,	juicy	granny.
9. At school	my	delightful,	polite,	warm	wizard	chased	the teacher's	small,	red	lunch.
10. In the park	my friend's		prickly,	wheezy	witch	smashed	my friend's	delicious,	purple	pet.
11. I heard that	Mum's	beautiful,	fuzzy,	scatty	teddy	hid	my	nutty,	silly	lunch.
12. I read that	my sister's	cheeky,	happy,	shaky	horse	captured	Grandad's	squeaky,	sleepy	brother.
13. ___ said	the	clever,	jolly,	smart	cat	gobbled	a	grumpy,	scary	sister.
14. I know	my brother's	clumsy,	lazy,	tidy	rabbit	chased	your	polite,	round	sandwich.
15. I think	Granny's	crazy,	mad,	tired	robot	painted	the teacher's	friendly,	cuddly	dragon.
16. Did you know	my friend's	dopey,	noisy,	troubled	sister	sold	my	soft,	white	horse?
17. Who said	your	dull,	nosy,	tricky	wizard	loved	Mum's	spotty,	black	friend?
18. Is it true	the teacher's	excited,	quiet,	warm	brother	ate	Granny's	smelly,	green	bun?
19. Did you hear	Grandad's	funny,	rude,	wet	mouse	frightened	my brother's	big,	yellow	book?
20. I know why	our	fussy,	scary,	wrinkly	elephant	burnt	your	small,	pink	pet.

MY SPELL-WELL RECORD

Week	1	2	3	4	5	6	7	8	9	10	11	12	13	14	15	16	17	18	19	20	21	22	23	24	25	26	27	28	29	30
1.																														
2.																														
3.																														
4.																														
5.																														
6.																														
7.																														
8.																														
9.																														
10.																														

1–6 ⭐ Trying hard! 7–9 ⭐ Well done! 10 ⭐ Super speller!